INSIDE THE EU BUSINESS ASSOCIATIONS

Also by Justin Greenwood

The Effectiveness of EU Business Associations (edited)
Representing Interests in the European Union
Social Partnership in the European Union (edited with Hugh Compston)
Organised Business and the New Global Order (edited with Henry Jacek)
Collective Action in the European Union (edited with Mark Aspinwall)
European Casebook on Business Alliances
Organised Interests and the European Community (edited with Jürgen Grote and Karsten Ronit)

Inside the EU
Business Associations

Justin Greenwood

palgrave

First published 2002 by
PALGRAVE
Houndmills, Basingstoke, Hampshire RG21 6XS and
175 Fifth Avenue, New York, N.Y. 10010
Companies and representatives throughout the world

PALGRAVE is the new global academic imprint of
St. Martin's Press LLC Scholarly and Reference Division and
Palgrave Publishers Ltd (formerly Macmillan Press Ltd).

ISBN 0–333–79376–5

This book is printed on paper suitable for recycling and
made from fully managed and sustained forest sources.

A catalogue record for this book is available
from the British Library.

Library of Congress Cataloging-in-Publication Data

Greenwood, Justin
    Inside the EU business associations / Justin Greenwood.
      p. cm.
    "Ernst & Young Association Management."
    Includes bibliographical references and index.
    ISBN 0–333–79376–5 (cloth)
      1. Trade associations—European Union Countries. I. Ernst & Young
Association Management. II. Title.
    HD2429.E87 G74 2001
    380.1'06'04—dc21   2001045864

10   9   8   7   6   5   4   3   2   1
11 10 09 08 07 06 05 04 03 02

Printed and bound in Great Britain by
Antony Rowe Ltd, Chippenham, Wiltshire

To Jill, Lucy and Anna

Contents

List of Tables*

---

*All tables drawn from original data collection have percentages rounded up or down to nearest per cent.

Acknowledgements

This is the ninth[1] book project I have completed in as many years on transnational (mainly EU) interest representation, though only my second as a single-authored manuscript. It is the first of my books wholly dedicated to my principal research interest, EU business interest associations, and the most research intensive of all, by a long distance. I am pleased to thank those who provided resources to enable primary data collection among 50 EU business associations, and 150 members and non-members of these associations. These were: Ernst & Young Association Management; the Confederation of Food and Drink Industries of the EU; Cargill plc; The Carnegie Trust for the Universities of Scotland; Pioneer Overseas Corporation; CBMC – Brewers of Europe; EURELECTRIC – Union of the Electricity Industry; the National Federation of Roofing Contractors (UK); EAAA – European Advertising Agencies Association; GIC Association Management; the Market Research Society (UK); and the British Academy, for financial support for conference attendance to help disseminate the results. I am also grateful to my employer, the Robert Gordon University, who provided me with an eight-month sabbatical from September 1998 to April 1999 to collect most of the data. These resources of time and money enabled me to undertake around 60 per cent of all the interviews undertaken for the project, and to employ the team of 11 other researchers who undertook interviews with members of EU business associations. To them I am grateful also.

Many organisations and individuals have been extremely generous in providing me with their time and information. I want to thank them all, particularly the EU business associations and their members who participated in the research, and to record my regret that they are too numerous to mention.

Most of all, my thanks go to the staff of Ernst & Young Association Management for their support and encouragement through much of the project, and in particular to Alfons Westgeest, Wills Hughes-Wilson and Bruno Alves. I hope this work brings deserved credit to them, and I thank them for hosting the launch of the book in Brussels.

JUSTIN GREENWOOD

---

[1] Includes one journal special issue.

List of Abbreviations

ACE	Alliance for Beverage Cartons and the Environment
ACEA	European Automobile Constructors Association
AEA	Association of European Airlines
AECM	European Independent Business Association
AECMA	European Association of Aerospace Industries
AIM	European Brands Association
AMCHAM-EU	EU Committee of the American Chamber of Commerce
AMUE	Association for the Monetary Union of Europe
BAR	Brussels Automobile Representatives
CAOBISCO	Association of the Chocolate Biscuit and Confectionery Industries of the EU
CBMC	Brewers of Europe
CEA	European Insurance Committee
CEA-PME	European Confederation of Associations of Small and Medium-Sized Enterprises
CEDI	European Confederation of Independents
CEE	Central and Eastern European
CEEP	Centre for Enterprises with Public Participation
CEFIC	European Chemicals Industry Council
CEMBUREAU	European Cement Industry Association
CEO	Chief Executive Officer
CEPS	European Confederation of Spirits Producers
CIAA	Confederation of the Food and Drink Industries of the EU
CIMSCEE	Committee of the Mustard Industries in the European Economic Community
COCERAL	Committee of Cereals, Oilseeds, Animal Feed, Olive Oil. Oils & Fats & Agrosupply Trade in the EU
COGECA	General Committee of Agricultural Cooperation in the EC
COLIPA	European Cosmetic Toiletry & Perfumery Association
CONCAWE	The Oil Companies' European Organisation for Environmental and Health Protection

COPA	Committee of Agricultural Organisations in the EC
CPIV	Standing Committee of the European Glass Industries
EAAA	European Advertising Agencies Association
EACEM	European Association of Consumer Electronic Manufacturers
EAIC	European–American Industrial Council
EASA	European Advertising Standards Alliance
EAT	European Advertising Tripartite
EBU	European Banking Union
EBU	European Broadcasting Union
EC	European Community
ECIS	European Centre for Infrastructure Studies
ECA	European Carpet Association
ECF	European Coffee Federation
ECIS	European Committee for Interoperable Software
ECSA	European Community Shipowners Association
EDA	European Dairy Association
EEC	European Economic Community
EEO	European Express Organisation
EFA	European Driving Schools Association
EFCA	European Federation of Consulting Engineers
EICTA	European Information and Communications Technologies Association
EFPIA	European Federation of Pharmaceutical Industry Associations
EGTA	European Group of Television Advertisers
EMOTA	European Mail Order Traders Association
EMSU	European Medium and Small Business Union
ERT	European Round Table of Industrialists
ESBA	European Small Business Alliance
ESCHFÖ	European Federation of Chimney Sweeps
ESNBA	European Secretariat of National Bioindustry Associations
ETRTO	European Tyre and Rim Technical Organisation
ETUC	European Trade Union Confederation
EU	European Union
EURATEX	European Apparel and Textile Organisation
EURELECTRIC	Union of the Electricity Industry
EUROCHAMBRES	Association of European Chambers of Commerce and Industry
EURO CHLOR	European Chlorine Association

EUROCOMMERCE	European Federation of Retailing and Distribution
EUROFER	European Confederation of Iron and Steel Industries
EUROPABIO	European Association for Bioindustries
EUROPECHE	Association of National Organisations of Fishing Enterprises in the EEC
EUROPIA	European Petroleum Industries Association
EUROFER	European Confederation of Iron and Steel Industries
FAEP	European Federation of Magazine Publishers
FIEC	European Construction Industry Federation
FPB	Forum of Private Business
FT	*Financial Times*
HOTREC	Confederation of the National Hotel and Restaurant Associations in the European Community
IFIEC	International Federation of Industrial Energy Consumers
IFPMA	International Federation of Pharmaceutical Manufacturers' Associations
IPSA	International Political Science Association
NIE	New Institutional Economics
NORMAPME	European Office of Craft and Small and Medium-Sized Enterprises for Standardisation
OBI	Organisation of Business Interests
ORGALIME	Liaison Group of the Mechanical, Electrical, Electronic and Metalworking Industries
PRSI	Pay Related Social Insurance
QMV	Qualified Majority Voting
SAGB	Senior Advisory Group Biotechnology
SAGE	Software Action Group for Europe
SME	Small and Medium-Sized Enterprises
TABD	Transatlantic Business Dialogue
TCE	Transaction Cost Economics
TENs	Trans-European Networks
TIE	Toy Industries of Europe
UASG	UNICE Advisory and Support Group
UEAPME	European Association of Craft, Small and Medium-Sized Enterprises
UNICE	Union of Industrial and Employers' Confederations of Europe
VÖI	Association of Austrian Industrialists
WKÖ	Austrian Federal Economic Chamber
WPG	White Paper on Governance
WTO	World Trade Organisation
ZDH	Zentralverband des Deutschen Handwerks

Exhibit 1 Building common platforms in a large Brussels-based EU business association. [Note in particular the translation facilities, including the window cubicles.]

1 Introduction

There are approximately 950 business interest associations organised at the EU level and formally constituted in law, accounting for around two-thirds of all EU formal interest organisations. This book is intended for those interested in:

- whether, and how, these organisations can be strong and cohesive players on the European stage;
- how the EU environment affects the capacities of business interest associations; and
- why EU business interest associations vary in their cohesiveness.

It presents fresh results, drawn from a unique data-set consisting of 49 interviews conducted with EU business associations and 151 conducted with their members, undertaken between 1998 and 2001, and from a wide-ranging review of the literature on business interest associations and EU interest representation. It is a contribution to a number of new and contemporary debates of concern both to analysts of European integration and business interest associations, and to those who work in and with EU business associations. It seeks to be accessible to all these types of readers, whether 'academic' or 'practitioner'.

Indeed, the study of EU business interest associations is more than a specialist pursuit best left to enthusiasts, or even a narrow concern limited to those who work in and with these organisations. Beyond the 'anorak' wonder of when, for instance, the European Natural Sausage Casing Association (ENSCA) was formed, how many staff are employed by the European Federation of Chimney Sweeps (ESCHFÖ) or, more seriously, concern among associations, their members and their partners for effective industry representation, the study of EU business associations is important because of:

- The role cast for them in explaining how European integration comes about. Under what circumstances can EU business associations be dynamic agents of integration? What are the circumstances that limit their contribution and consequently challenge accounts of the integration process built upon their supposed contribution?
- The related debate about the circumstances under which business associations can be 'strong' organisations capable of a high degree of cohesion, able to meet the needs of their members and the institutions capable of being a coherent governance partner in public policy. More specifically, in terms suggested by Traxler (1991), how can they unify their members' interests and ensure the compliance of their members with these goals? How can they

develop the required autonomy to assume this role, that is to move away from being the reactive slaves of their members, tied to their short-term demands and lacking in flexibility to be governance partners, to being pro-active organisations? In this latter scenario, would an association typically lead perceptions among their members as to what their interests are, prioritising what they believe to be the long-term interests of members over their short-term demands?

- The link between 'governance' and economic performance, particularly in the context of the recent debate on 'European governance' launched by the European Commission. Do EU business associations distort markets, optimal wealth distribution and efficiencies by extracting special privileges from political authorities, or/and are they capable of performing wider public goals, such as the regulation of markets? and if so, in which circumstances? To what extent does the EU environment disable the potential utility and strength of EU associations in helping their members to lower the transaction costs of doing business by its strict rules on competition policy?
- Unresolved questions about what drives business interests to act together, the extent and circumstances under which membership is driven by incentives or is semi-automatic, and to what extent the 'EU' level imposes special dynamics upon these issues.
- Whether there is something in the make up of business interest associability at the EU level that adds to, or detracts from, the naturally 'privileged position' of business in politics. Business interest practitioners are frequently heard to complain that their industries are 'economic giants yet political dwarfs' in the EU, yet those in 'public interest groups' also complain that 'business rules' in the EU.

These agendas are the inspiration for this book. They follow an overview of the constituency of EU business interest associations provided by this first chapter. In this endeavour, the reader should note the focus in the first paragraph of this chapter; this book is about EU business interest associations that are formally constituted in law. Despite a plethora of other actors and channels in and through which business interests are represented, it is these organisations which, still, provide the mainstay of business interest representation that is addressed to and channelled through the EU level. Indisputably, much business interest representation may still be channelled through national outlets, and there are differing views as to whether most of it goes via 'EU', 'national' or 'regional' channels. Similarly, business interests are certainly represented at the EU level by actors including companies, national associations, representatives of regional authorities, or informal networks of varying types. However, this book seeks to be a specialist focus upon business interest associations organised at and addressed to the EU level, and formally constituted in law. The activities (or lack of them) of other actors in the kaleidoscope of EU interest representation is only considered in so far as they impact upon EU-level formal business interest associations.

All EU business associations have a common environment in the political system of the EU. This system exerts common influences upon their performance, and it is a task of this book to describe and analyse them, and to indicate the extent to which the EU environment places special influences upon the capacities of EU business associations. Variations in the EU environment can also be used to help explain variations in the capacities of EU business associations. Indeed, the principle task of this book is to identify those factors that create variation in the capacities of EU business interest associations, and it is this endeavour that absorbs much of the intellectual energy of this book. These are questions that will interest scholars, practitioners and consumers of business interest associations in any setting, EU or otherwise. To assist this diverse readership, the remainder of this first chapter is devoted to describing the principle features of EU business interest associations.

EU BUSINESS INTEREST ASSOCIATIONS IN OVERVIEW

Head Counts

There have been few head counts of EU-level interest associations. My own estimate of around 950 EU business associations contrasts with a figure supplied by Gray, based on a single directory source, indicating a total of around 660 in 1997 (Gray, 1998: 284). In the main, analysts have been left to draw assumptions from figures supplied for the entire population of interests organised at the European level, whether these groups organise business, workers or public interests. Apart from the first of these exercises, in which Butt Philip (1985) produced one of the very first informed estimates in 1985 of 525 groups, these tend to have obscured rather than assisted the 'head count' game. In 1998, Gray included among his count of 1885 'EU pressure groups' categories such as consultants, conferences, think-tanks, law firms, corporate EU offices and national associations. More frequently cited is a claim originating from a 1992 Commission document that there are 'approximately 3000 special interest groups of varying types in Brussels' (Commission, 1992: 4). This 'headline' figure has found its way into folklore as a result both of the frequency with which it has been repeated, and because of the superficially definitive nature of the source. There is, however, considerable scope for caution. Firstly, the source document itself is ambiguous. Two sentences on from the '3000 special interest groups' assertion comes the statement that 'within this total there are more than 500 European and international federations', thus implying that the remainder are aggregations of interests other than those organised at the European level. Secondly, it was a 'back of envelope' type calculation. The division within the Secretariat General of the European Commission responsible for the document produced the figure of 3000 by making a number of educated guesses. It was derived from assumptions about the approximate size of a number of different segments of the interest group community, with a certain amount of doubling, and doubling again. It had never been intended as a definitive figure to be cited and re-cited, and indeed some years later in 1996 this same division of the Commission published a directory listing of all the EU-level groups of which it was aware, producing a figure of 700 such groups. Even at that point, some four years after the '3000 interest groups' document, the Commission division viewed its figure of 700 as somewhat experimental, hoping it would prompt information about groups not included to be forthcoming (European Commission, 1996).

The author offers a current figure of 1398 EU level groups, of which 951 (68%) are business associations, compiled from a composite database of EU-level groups derived from six Directory sources, as well as the continuing 'radar' sources of the author. Directory sources include those published by (in order of importance of use) EurActiv.com (2001), Landmarks (2000 edition of the *European Public Affairs Directory*), Euroconfidentiel (1999 edition of the *Directory of 9300 Trade and Professional Associations in the European Community*), European Commission (2001, internet), the Union of International Associations (1998), and Butt Philip and Gray (1996). 'Radar' sources include continuing contact with those who work in and with EU business interest associations, as well as public sources such as the 'situations vacant' columns of the weekly newspaper *European Voice*, which yields a steady supply of organisations that do not appear in directory sources.

Delivering a figure such as the one offered above always requires fine judgements over 'borderline cases' with other categories, such as organisations representing the interests of particular categories of workers, most notably those providing professional services. Should, for instance, organisations seeking to represent the interests of professionals engaged in business services, such as architects, accountants and lawyers, be classified as 'organisations representing the professions', or 'business interest organisations?' Even seemingly straightforward cases, such as organisations representing the likes of self-employed chimney sweeps, are defined by those representing them at the EU level as 'organisations representing the professions' rather than business organisations (UEAPME, 1998). There are no easy solutions to the complexities of these shades of 'grey' cases. The very question of 'what is a 'profession' is itself highly vexed and disputed, let alone the particularly problematic borderline between business services and the professions. The best the author can offer is some transparency for the judgements arrived at, and to resort to the 'elephant' judgement of knowing something when it is encountered without always being able to define it precisely. This has been to treat indisputably professional service organisations (for example architects, accountants and lawyers) as a distinct category of 'professions'. This is because they are set apart from business because of their mixed public and private sector composition and service orientation, their independent basis of governance, and the 'feel' factor suggests that their interests are challenged as much by legislation aimed at the freedom of movement of labour and of establishment than by general business legislation. This 'feel' factor suggests that examples such as organisations representing chimney sweeps, on the other hand, are more appropriately treated as a business interest organisation because their interests are more impacted by business environment legislation than that aimed specifically at the professions. Another question again concerns that of farmers. Should representative organisations of farmers be included in a headcount of business interest associations? For headcount purposes farmers, are treated as agri-business, because most are also engaged in for-profit activities, with the remainder organised in co-operatives who, whilst a mixed profit orientation group, have interests engaged in ownership of production and commercial transactions.

Whilst comparable figures over time for EU-level business interest associations are not available, numbers appear to have stabilised from a plateau level reached in the mid-1990s when much of the single-market programme had been achieved. Because approaching 80 per cent of all economic and labour market legislation passing through member-state legislatures originates from Brussels (UNICE, 2001), few business interest domains by the present time do not have a representative EU association. However, as is evident from the discussion below, the landscape of associations is by no means static, with new associations emerging as a result of changing business and sectoral conditions.

Location

Belgium has been a friendly environment to international organisations since long before the creation of the European Economic Community, with a key item of legislation passed shortly after the First World War aimed at facilitating their establishment by a country geographically well-placed to do so. The Belgian Law on international associations, of 25 October 1919, was passed in the immediate aftermath of the most destructive war known to mankind, in the spirit of promoting European co-operation and fraternity. This helps explain the establishment of a number of organisations with international missions in Brussels, including the Union of International Associations. For EU associations, it has made the task of setting up in the most obvious location that much easier.

Given this, it is something of a surprise, at first glance, that less than two-thirds (62% – 589) of all EU business associations are based in Belgium. Mostly, these are located in Brussels, with the remainder highly disbursed throughout the member states (Table 1.1). This proportion is slightly lower than might be intuitive, and requires some analysis and explanation:

1　It is an identical proportion to that of public interests (62% of valid sample – 149), the second-largest category (19% – 266) of EU interest associations. While business interests do have a superior resource base when taken as a whole, public interest groups have a variety of EU funding and other initiatives aimed at attracting them to Brussels. A small number, particularly the environmental organisations, have a substantial resource base of their own to draw upon.

2　Belgium is a high-wage economy with high levels of employment protection for workers, meaning that associations representing members with a low resource potential, without the possibility to attract public subsidies, may be deterred from coming to Brussels.

3　EU associations are young, on a relatively low resource base in comparison to their national counterparts (see Chapter 3), and have not had the opportunity to build up the reserves required to purchase their premises. Entering the Brussels property market rather late in the day, they are victims of high property prices rather than beneficiaries of it. This resource limitation has implications for their autonomy, which is examined further in Chapter 6.

4　If EU-level associations based within 2.5 hours travel distance by land from Brussels are included, then the proportion rises to over 75 per cent of all business associations, whereas the remaining public interest group bases are more geographically disbursed. These additional business organisations are based in the Paris, Bonn and Hague/Amsterdam conurbations, sometimes originating from international business organisations (also typical of those based in Paris and The Hague), and sometimes existing alongside the offices of domestic business interest associations (typical of those based in Bonn and Amsterdam). The remaining 25 per cent of EU business interest associations, outside of all of these locations, differ significantly in profile from business sectors represented by associations in Brussels, in that they are either less-significant economic players, or the constituent firm size is small. A significant proportion of these do operate from the offices of domestic business interest associations, often as a result of low availability of resources. For these associations who operate from the offices of their members, the over dependence upon the resources of their host results in a lack of autonomy. As is discussed in more detail in Chapter 5, the degree of autonomy of an association from its membership is a key factor in the strength and capacity of associations to contribute to public policy governance.

The dispersion of EU business associations by country of location is recorded in Table 1.1.

Table 1.1 EU business interest associations:
country of location

Country of location	Number	%
Belgium	589	62
France	80	8
Germany	73	8
Italy	19	2
Luxembourg	14	1
Netherlands	41	4
Switzerland	22	2
UK	52	5
Other	61	6
Total	951	100[*]

[*]Rounded up or down proportions.
Sources: EurActiv (2001); Euroconfidentiel (1999); European Commission (2001); Landmarks (2001); Union of International Associations (1998).

Diversity and Domain

Every interest categorised by Standard Industrial Classification (SIC) is organised at the European level. The overwhelming majority are 'trade' or 'sector-specific' associations, with a good many organised at the sub-sectoral level. A high degree of specialism is apparent, with associations dedicated to the representation of such entities as natural sausage casings, caramel producers, herbal infusion drinks, chewing-gum manufacture and ostrich farmers. In many cases this specialisation reflects industry fragmentation or divisions in the product chain, which make it easier for businesses to operate in highly specialised associations where the membership constituency is small and interests similar, allowing the association to operate coherently. Hence, there are specialised associations in the glass sector representing the interests of firms producing container glass, flat glass, glass fibres, technical glass or cut glass, as well as a standing committee of the glass industries. In some cases the specialism is more apparent than real, in that some association names conjuring images of rural artisans churning out specialised products mask the reality of an organisation which is a multinational food processing company in a highly concentrated industry 'family'.

Hence, associations representing mustards, mayonnaise and condiments, dehydrated fruits, vegetable proteins, fruits and vegetables in brine, cider and fruit wines, tomato processors and dessert mixes, all operate from the same address in Brussels as the frozen-food products association and the fish processors association, in which the multinational company Unilever features prominently. Many of these associations are constructed as an association of national associations with identical constitutions and annual general meetings held on the same day, although in most cases the same company dominates the national association. In this way, a single entity can appear to be acting collectively, perhaps responding to a preference of the EU institutions for collective European-level organisations.

The apparent stabilisation of numbers of EU business interest associations should not, however, mask a small number of interesting developments. Hence, the European Modern Restaurants Association (EMRA) is a 'virtual' organisation representing the interests of high-street fast-food chains such as McDonalds, Burger King and Pizza Hut, using modern technologies and resource sharing (including Belgian corporate premises of members) to avoid the need for traditional associational infrastructure such as buildings and a permanent secretariat. Since its emergence in 1998 as an organisation dedicated to a previously unrepresented collective interest, there have been few signs of this organisation developing into a more traditional structure. Another expression of change is provided by the European Information and Communication Technologies Association (EICTA), a result of a merger between a telecoms and IT association to reflect changing sectoral definitions as a result of new technologies. These two examples are indicative of trends that will continue to deliver some change in the constituency of EU business interest associations in the years to come, as change agents deliver changes to sectoral definition and the crystallisation of sub-sectoral interests.

These examples illustrate the fluidity and difficulties involve in defining what is a 'sector', and the extent to which many associations do not seek to position themselves as encompassing representatives of a 'sector'. Apart from specialisms by type of industrial activities, there are also associations specialising in highly specific types of issues. For instance, the Alliance for Beverage Cartons and the Environment (ACE), is a highly specific association representing the interests of carton and beverage container manufacturers, such as Tetra-Pak, in environmental policy-making. Others represent issues across sectors, such as the branded products association AIM (European Brands Association) which represents the interests of manufacturers of all proprietary products (such as washing powders, designer labels etc.) *vis-à-vis* the purchasing power of large retailers and the intellectual property issues that arise with 'generics' manufacturers. This is quite typical for systems of interest representation as a whole. Associations may also have unwritten agreements with others to specialise in 'issue niches' so as not to compete with one another for members (see Browne, 1990), and seek to acquire reputations as the organisation to join for particular sets of issues.

In consequence, there are associations representing specialist issues, sub-sectoral interests, those that seek to correspond roughly to sectoral interests, while others quite deliberately seek authority as representatives across a very broad spectrum of business activities, territories or of a particular type of firm size. For instance, the Union of Industrial and Employers' Confederations of Europe (UNICE) seeks to represent all European business and employer interests; and the EU Committee of the American Chamber of Commerce (AMCHAM-EU) seeks to represent the interests of 'European firms of American parentage'. The European Association of Craft, Small and Medium-Sized Enterprises (UEAPME) positions itself as the cross-sectoral small-business representative (although its position as 'the voice of small business' is disputed by other, smaller organisations, while UNICE regularly claims that its derivative constituency is 90 per cent small and medium-sized enterprises (SMEs)). The European Round Table of Industrialists (ERT) invites the Chief Executive Officers (CEOs) of a select number (presently, 46[1]) of Europe's largest companies into its membership, although this latter organisation is more of a 'big-issue think tank' than an association focusing on everyday issues in public affairs. EUROCHAMBRES, the Association of European Chambers of Commerce and Industry, represents national and local chambers of commerce Europe-wide, although as is discussed later it lacks the authority and recognition of these other organisations. Nonetheless, it shares with UNICE an impressively wide geographical scope of country members (numbering in the mid-30s), and, in common with many other business associations, has for some time admitted members from outside of EU member states from both applicant and non-applicant countries. In addition to this complexity, the formats of these organisations differ between those organising associations, firms, individuals or, in the case of other associations, some combination of these. These organisations are described and assessed later in this chapter.

Format

Most EU business interest associations have a membership constituency of either national associations, or large companies, or both. Much of the pattern of this can be explained by the structure of the industry, in that sectors dominated

---

[1] For a current list of members see the organisations web site at www.ert.be

by small firms tend to be represented by associations of national associations, whereas highly concentrated sectors tend to be represented by direct company membership organisations. A small number admit other EU associations into membership, and very few organise individuals in the business community. Many have different membership categories in which one or more of these types of members are admitted into full membership, with others holding some form of associate membership.

Whilst precise figures for association format type are not available for the constituency of 951 business groups, an informal random sample of 200 associations drawn from a directory listing (Euroconfidentiel, 1999) undertaken by the author suggests that the most common type is the association of national associations (58% – 116), followed by associations that organise both national associations and companies direct (26% – 52), followed by the direct company membership-only format (16% – 32). The latter are fewer in number because these exist almost exclusively in business sectors that are populated by large firm members who have the resources to fund a dedicated EU-level association. It is these types of actors – large firms – which have been the greatest change agent for EU business interest associations since the start of the single-market project, and over time there has been a distinct trend for EU associations to admit companies directly into some form of membership category. Before 1985, the overwhelming majority of EU business interest associations were associations of national associations, that is federations. Since 1985, many large firms have become active in EU public affairs by funding a permanent presence in Brussels (by 2001, around 250), and it is this stimulus to which federations have responded. Many of the federations found their positions and status being undermined by the dialogue which company public affairs offices in Brussels developed with the EU institutions, and sought to incorporate these firms within their structures. One model has been to hold a regular series of meetings with the Brussels-based managers of these offices in an attempt to coordinate positions. Another model has been to include companies within the membership structure of associations, whether as full members or as some type of associate members. For the national association members this route has been fraught with controversy because it means a dilution of their control and influence and some loss of their autonomy *vis-à-vis* their members, who may adopt the possibility of monitoring the activities of their national association and influencing their voting positions as they sit alongside them in the decision-making structures of EU associations. For EU federation secretariats, however, the admission of companies into some form of membership category offers the prospect of enhancing their resource base and their own autonomy by reducing their dependence upon one category of members. Consequently, a typical pattern has been for EU federation secretariats to seek the admission of large firms directly into membership, resisted by national association members. Almost always, these moves have been accompanied by a high degree of conflict.

An example of these types of conflicts is provided by the decision of UNICE to create an Advisory and Support Group (UASG) of large firms in 1990. UNICE has always represented national associations of business, and like other organisations in this position is always vulnerable to the criticism from public institutions that it lacks knowledge at the sharp end of business experience and is something akin to an industrial civil service. Consequently, the then General Secretary of UNICE, Zygmunt Tyszkiewicz, proposed the establishment of UASG to help establish closer links with business practice, and to diversify the fiscal, expertise and support base of the association. Despite the proposal falling well short of seeking the admission of firms into a voting category of membership alongside national associations, it met with some resistance from the national association members. The outcome was an agreement that the UASG would provide a maximum of 25 per cent of the resources of the association. UASG presently includes 26 firms,[2] and the presence of non-European firms such as Coca-Cola, Esso, Mars and Time Warner indicates the extent to which this proposal was driven by resource needs rather than a preemptive move to introduce company membership through the back door. Yet, given such tensions in seeking to create a non-voting advisory and support group of large companies, the reader will not be surprised at some of the bloodletting that has accompanied proposals in other European federations to admit companies into full membership alongside national association members. Where the issue has arisen but not been resolved, the result has usually been for national association members to seek to increase their control over the activities of their secretariat, and the General Secretary in particular, resulting in a loss of autonomy for the association and a consequent loss of ability to act as an effective governance partner with public authorities. In some cases known to the author, national associations have forbidden the General Secretary of the European association to communicate with companies in the sector other than through the national associations. In others, the tension has resulted in the end of the relationship between the General Secretary and the association.

Activities

In general, EU associations have a much narrower range of activities than their national counterparts. This is because they originate from the need amongst

---

[2] The members are listed in Table 5.1 in Chapter 5.

their members to find political representation at the European level. National associations do not need a comprehensive range of membership services from their European federation, but primarily seek political representation and information to enable them, in turn, to fulfil the needs of their own members at the national level. As is discussed later, national associations are by nature political animals whose *raison d'être* is representation, and they do not tend to require a range of special incentives to entice them into membership. Something similar applies in the case of direct member associations, whose large-firm members do not need a comprehensive range of special membership incentives, such as discounted services. The role of EU associations therefore contrasts sharply with national associations who provide a comprehensive range of membership services in response to the perceived needs of their members, such that in some cases political representation is almost a 'byproduct' of a service-based membership organisation. Consequently, EU business associations tend to have much smaller secretariat sizes than is common at the national level.

This restricted basis of EU associations is significant for the debate about whether membership is driven by incentives, or is semi-automatic. If EU associations are primarily concerned with the political interests of their members, so the incentives are concerned with access to this work (such as representation and information) and the network organisation. Where membership arises through incentives, it may be driven by the positive goods produced by an association, such as its reputation for lobbying, information and analysis, and the quality of the network, or for the quite different perspective of needing to be in a position to exert influence over the work of the association. On the other hand, there may be no 'reason' for membership at all, other than it is 'the thing to do', or habit. These issues may also vary according to whether the membership 'decision' is whether to join, or whether to continue in membership, and in the latter scenario there may be very little that resembles anything like a 'decision' in that continued membership may occur through inertia.

Resources and Secretariat

Although resource levels of EU associations in general can be expected to be lower than those of associations in the member states because of their narrow focus upon political representation, their nature and sources can still reveal much about the degree of autonomy of an association from its members, the extent to which it is dependent upon its members, and the distribution of influence between members. Whilst there is no comprehensive data source available, the author's own research sources yield a number of useful indications.

My own data taken in the mid-1990s, drawn from a postal questionnaire among 224 associations, indicated a median secretariat size of 3–3.5 full-time equivalent[3] staff, with a majority having a turnover in excess of €100 000. Of this sample 7 per cent (15) had no staff at all, while 20 per cent (30) had a turnover of less than €20 000. These latter organisations tend to be overdependent upon their members for resources, and in consequence lack the autonomy required of governance partners. At the other extreme, 13 per cent (30) had more than 10 staff. Easily the largest association is the European Chemicals Industry Council (CEFIC) which, together with a 'family' of specialist chemical associations under its umbrella structure, employs in excess of 120 staff. Around 80 of these are dedicated to the specific needs of the CEFIC parent. CEFIC, embracing a 'three-pillar' structure of membership in equal proportion (national associations, European associations, companies) is unusually large among the constituency of EU associations.

The next-largest organisations in terms of staff size are COPA/COGECA (Committee of Agricultural Organisations in the EU/General Committee of Agricultural Cooperation in the EU), with a secretariat size in the mid-50s, followed by UNICE, with 48 staff. Next come a clutch of associations with a secretariat size ranging between 20–35, including (in descending order) EFPIA (European Federation of Pharmaceutical Industry Associations), EURELECTRIC – Union of the Electricity Industry, CIAA (Confederation of the Food and Drink Industries of the EU), EUROFER (European Confederation of Iron and Steel Industries), CEMBUREAU (European Cement Industry Association), Euro-Commerce (representing retail, wholesale and distributive trades), AMCHAM-EU, and ACEA (European Automobile Constructors Association). Some of these organisations have slimmed down in size in recent years in response to contraction of the industries they represent, such as EUROFER, and CEMBUREAU. Others have grown and developed in proportion to the development of EU regulatory activity, such as EURELECTRIC – Union of the Electricity Industry.

Secretariat size should not be seen as a predictor on its own of associational strength, particularly in the case of organisations which are not tied to one particular sector. For instance, EUROCHAMBRES and EuroCommerce are among the better-resourced EU associations in staff numbers, yet do not enjoy a reputation on the Brussels scene as strong and coherent associations. Paradoxically, the business organisation with one of the strongest reputations, the European Round Table of Industrialists (ERT) has one of the leanest organisations, operating from modest premises with a secretariat of seven staff. Whilst the ERT is not comparable to other operational business associations for the reasons outlined earlier, it does demonstrate how an organisation which is dependent upon the resources of its members – whether status, expertise or fiscal – can also be influential. Similarly,

---

[3] All the figures given for staff numbers in this section are for full-time-equivalent staff working under the operational direction of the association.

AMCHAM-EU is also a membership-driven organisation, whose 135 members and associate members (service providers, led by public affairs consultancies) provide for a teeming structure of working parties and committees bursting with life. The expertise and authority of the senior industry figures involved in this work account for the high regard in which the organisation is held. Whilst AMCHAM-EU has a secretariat of 20 or so staff, this total is relatively small in relation to the range of functions it undertakes. Whereas in some organisations the principal–agent (here, member–secretariat) relationship has become confused in the inevitable search for control by bureaucracies, in AMCHAM-EU much of the work is undertaken by members, with staff playing a supportive background role. The challenge that these examples provide to the importance of trade association autonomy for the cohesion and strength of the organisation is discussed in Chapter 5.

The source of secretariat staff is a further indication of its strength. Here, the key quality is independence. If association staff are seconded by members rather than employed centrally, that in turn may reduce associational autonomy by increasing dependence upon members. Associations need a supply of expertise they can call their own (Coleman, 1985), and the development and monopolisation of that expertise, and the extent to which the association can make its public policy partners and members dependent upon it, may be key to associational autonomy. One indication of this is the presence of functional divisions within the association which focus upon particular specialisms. For instance, EURELECTRIC-Union of the Electricity Industry has functional divisions covering generation and transmission; distribution and supply; energy policy; market regulation; the environment and sustainable development; and management practices (covering a specialised organisational issue in that industry) – as well as administrative divisions spanning communications, information technology, and administration/logistics. A further dimension of this is trust in the independence of staff, which encourages use of an association by its members.

Member subscription levels in EU associations vary with all these factors. Some research conducted among a (self-selecting) sample of 135 UK associations in 1997 indicated a reported range of subscription fees to EU associations from 0 through to €800 000, though with a relatively low median of €7581 (Compass Partnership, 1997). For most of the medium to large EU associations employing in excess of 20 staff, a typical subscription for a national association is likely to be around €150 000. While there are exceptions, affiliation fees for direct-membership associations tend on the whole to be less per unit, because these organisations are just one among a number of public affairs strategies employed by large firms, and consequently the representative organisations tend on the whole to be smaller. One very large national high-street retailer, for instance, pays just €5 000 to be a member of its principal EU association, while a multinational healthcare firm which maintains eight affiliations to industrial associations pays an average of €40 000. The irony is that membership fee levels are much less price-sensitive among the very large firms who dominate the membership of direct-member associations; as one public affairs manager of a company affiliating to ten EU associations told the author, 'the amounts involved are peanuts. If it cost more, we'd pay more'. Many large firms are happy to pay a disproportionate share of the costs involved in running the association in return for a greater degree of influence, and in many associations there are unwritten, and sometimes written, rules in which votes and subscription fees are weighted. In one cross-sectoral association, for instance, the largest association pays an annual subscription of €115 000, while the smallest pays less than €20 000. Despite each of these having the same voting rights in the formal structure of the association, in common with many associations the practice is not to vote, and consequently platform-building in the association is informally tilted towards the largest subscriber, although perhaps not in relation to the differences in fees paid. Larger members, on the whole, tend to accept their responsibilities for leading political action in the domains in which they operate in, and find that their ability to find their own views expressed in the collective name of the association is worth the investment.

Over time, there has been a change in the typical national composition of leadership of EU associations. Guéguen recently attributed a haemorrhage of French-speaking personnel from among the ranks of General Secretaries of EU associations to the introduction of the TGV service between Paris and Brussels, with easy daytime commuting providing French public affairs candidates with access to similar careers with French-based organisations (Guéguen, 2000). Over time, there has certainly been a loss of French nationals to the leading positions of EU business associations, though there is an historical legacy of French influence in EU associations in that two-thirds of EU associations still bear a French language name. Guéguen, himself a Frenchman and onetime General Secretary, detects a switch to Belgian, Dutch, British and German nationals (*ibid.*). Boléat remarks that EU associations tend to be dominated by German interests (Boléat, 1996), and whilst the status of Germany as the most populated country of Europe may explain some of this, there is a grain of truth to the claim that German associational interests are disproportionately represented in the world of EU associations.[4] In part, this is a function of the strength of the system of associations in Germanic systems of governance. German national associations are certainly very strongly represented amongst the national associations

---

[4] The first two EU associations named in this book, the European Natural Sausage Casing Association (ENSCA) and the European Federation of Chimney Sweeps (ESCHFO), are both German-based organisations. A good many of the very highly specialised EU associations are Germanic in origin, representing the culture of associative life in that country.

present in Brussels. Impressionistically, the author's interviews suggest also that German firms are more likely to view their EU associations as the mainstay of their representational strategies, while counterparts from countries where business representation is more pluralist seem to attach less emphasis to their associational membership, even where the firms concerned are from the same sector.

These differences in culture do contribute to the special difficulties of governability that many EU associations experience. Collaborative cultures vary in different European countries, with different dispensations from the outset towards 'trust' in others (Newton, 2001; see also Chapter 5). Language, too, is a problem for EU business associations that should not be underestimated. In Chapter 5, drawing on the work of one association, an illustrative indication is given of the sheer size of the workload involved in translating a huge number of documents and meetings that comprise the routine work of an EU business association (see also Exhibit 1, p. xvii). This consumes a significant proportion of the resources of EU business associations, and is a major disadvantage for them in comparison with associations in other settings. Boléat (1996) draws attention to wider implications, in that he suggests that decisions as to the personnel to participate in EU business associations, whether by members or the associations themselves, is overdominated by considerations of language ability rather than other considerations of merit. Boléat also signposts a wider issue in the debate on EU business associations, in that it has often been claimed that the General Secretary position has been a pre-retirement post, a consolation prize for an unsuccessful post-seeker elsewhere, or simply a convenient way of getting rid of someone. These points are raised here not by way of endorsement of them, but to identify some of the caricatures that are drawn of EU business associations. In the experience of the author, the challenge of platform-building in such a complicated and often difficult environment usually draws individuals of the highest calibre.

Nomenclature

A familiar point to any reader in the field is the different usage of terms by different sources. For instance, to some the terms 'interest group' or 'pressure group' denote any type of interest association, whereas to others these terms denote only public or citizen interests. Similarly, the term 'non-governmental organisation' (NGO) is fraught with confusion, with some writers using these terms to denote generic or specialised types of interests. Much the same is true of the world of business. Hence a final point in describing the landscape of EU-level formal business interest associations is a health warning about its own nomenclature. Authors, directory sources, business interests and others upon whom they have an impact use different terms to describe the phenomenon under investigation. Some of these derive from accepted usage in different cultures, but when terms are used in dialogue with those from other cultures they may convey other meanings. For instance, the term 'trade association' is commonly used in the UK as a generic term to denote all business interest associations. But when this term is used in conversation with those from other cultural settings, it may denote a highly specialist organisation whose main embrace is the transaction of goods for profit, that is commerce and the infrastructure involved in the exchange of goods. In this latter setting, the term 'trade' excludes those associations organising the interests of manufacturing and service industry. The term 'industry association' is also used in a generic and specialist way between and within different cultural settings. In some countries, business interest associations are commonly divided between employer and product market associations, whereas in others there is no distinction. Use of the term 'business interest association' may even denote the exclusion of 'employer' associations. In this book, the term 'business interest association' is used in an embracing and generic sense to denote all these activities, whether from the point of view of the employer of labour or not. An association organising a specific domain, whether sectoral or otherwise (sub-sectoral, or a specialism across sectors), is referred to as a 'domain-specific' association.

A further difficulty of nomenclature is provided by description of the cross-constituency business organisations. Some of the issues were indicated above in the section on 'diversity and domain', where the difficulty of conveying meaning through the term 'cross-sectoral' was evident together with the problems that arise in attempting to define what a 'sector' is. A number of associations, such as AIM and EuroCommerce, organise interests across sectors – whatever a 'sector' may be – and in that sense are 'cross-sectoral'. Neither of these organisations, however, is comparable to those organisations that seek to embrace the entire constituency of business interests. Hence, the phrase 'cross-sectoral' is invested with a number of different connotations and its use is fraught with difficulties. A smart term is required which clearly conveys reservation of meaning to all those organisations seeking to organise across the broad spectrum of business activities; here, the term 'constituency-wide' is the best offering that can be made. Even this term is qualified in that all business-wide organisations are, strictly speaking, limited in some way, whether by geographical territory (e.g. European or American business), format (associations, or direct membership organisations), or specialisms by firm size. A sub-section within this grouping is formed by the 'peak' organisations of business, those at the 'top layer' of business organisation which are federations of national cross constituency business associations. UNICE is the peak organisation of business at the EU level, although UEAPME and EUROCHAMBRES are clearly also legitimate members of the 'peak' club, despite the partiality in coverage of their constituencies. These organisations are referred to as 'business-wide' associations throughout this book.

Decision-making Structures

The formal decision-making structures of EU business associations have a ring of predictability about them. The 'engine houses' of building policy positions are the specialist working groups, usually operating by the authority of a number of functional policy committees – such as social affairs, environmental affairs, and so on. Typically, these then report to a further tier of authority, with someone – usually the General Secretary – entrusted with deciding whether positions can be issued straight away, or need to be discussed further in some other fora. Where referral is made, perhaps to an Executive Committee, that committee may, in turn, pass it to the highest decision-making body of the organisation for decision, perhaps because the members of the Executive are divided on the proposal. Once it reaches the supreme, plenary decision-making authority, there may be statutes designed to resolve situations in which members disagree, such as qualified majority voting with or without weighting. These structures are discussed further in Chapter 3 and again, through working examples, in Chapter 5, in which the implications of different decision-making structures for associational governability are assessed. In general, those associations that are designed for their breadth of representation have more decision-making tiers than those that are structures that are dedicated to representing an exclusive set of interests. The former organisations are geared towards authoritativeness of position by carrying the entire membership with them, whereas the latter are geared towards faster decision-making at a higher level of specificity. In general, federative structures (associations of associations) are better suited to the former purpose, while direct company membership is better suited to the latter.

This distinction explains the variation in the degree of 'flatness' of tiers of decision-making, ranging from those which can declare a working party position to be that of the association after its passage through just one further tier of authority, to those with up to seven tiers before something becomes the official position of the association. The first of these types is clearly well-geared to speed of decision-making, whereas the latter is geared towards rigour, consultation and consensus. The benefit of the former, speed, is offset by the lack of authoritativeness in being able to speak on behalf of all interests affected. The benefits of the latter, authoritativeness, bring with them a cost of longer decision-taking times, as well as a tendency towards lowest common denominator positions. The need for consensus also influences the culture of organisations, in that those based around consensus rarely vote and shy away from differential positions. Qualified majority voting (QMV) systems can sometimes be in place in the statutes in order to encourage members to reach a compromise.

Large-membership organisations also tend towards more tiers of decision-making in order to accommodate the sheer number of interests involved. Smaller organisations, on the other hand, comprising like-minded people from companies of a similar size (and often, therefore, interests) can rely more upon interpersonal relationships and a background of trust between members based on their repeated contacts. This quality – trust between members – is a key 'glue' that makes associations work, and it can be developed by social functions hosted by the association (Chapter 3). On the other hand, 'tourism associations' can irritate the more businesslike member representatives, particularly in those sectors where there is a high turnover of personnel and little chance of developing long-term relationships. This quality of trust is also influenced by the extent to which members are present in Brussels, although the cost of this is a loss of autonomy of the secretariat through increased monitoring by members, and an overdependence upon the membership for resources. In general, business-wide associations have proved most adept at using the resources of members present in Brussels to their advantage (Chapter 5), enhancing coordination, expertise and channels of communication with both the derivative membership in the member states and with the full range of national actors involved in the EU institutions.

Degrees of autonomy are also reflected in the role taken by the President and the role of the Board. These roles are somewhat underanalysed in the academic literature on business associations, but are heavily stressed in the practitioner 'grey literature' (see, for instance, Boléat, 2001; Macdonald, 2001). A variety of presidential systems can be found in EU business associations, including those based on rotation or open elections, with or without systems designed to ensure continuity (where the position of vice-president is given to those before and after taking the Presidency), or by election. As with the EU, a Presidency is a limited-life opportunity (in the case of UNICE, for two years, renewable once) to agenda set a number of issues. General Secretaries almost always allude to the importance of having a strong working relationship with a President, summed up by Boléat's (2001) sharp advice that the President and the Board need to be involved, but not too involved. An overinvolved President and/or Board can restrict the role of the General Secretary and other staff members to little more than administrative functionaries. In turn, this can have drastic consequences on the autonomy of an association, its ability to bring value to its members and to provide leadership to them, and ultimately the effectiveness of an association (Chapter 3). Given that a President and Board have the power of hiring and firing, the degree of 'space' and protection afforded to the General Secretary to take risks by leading its members, rather than being the simple servant of them, can be crucial. A President can do much to protect the General Secretary in this role. Whilst it is difficult to legislate for the personality factors that influence President/General Secretary relations, the statutes can do much to enable autonomy to flourish through constitutional definitions of the roles of postholders. Reading the statutes of organisations can reveal much about them, their design purpose, and their likely effectiveness (Chapter 5).

MAKING CONNECTIONS: THE DEBATES TO WHICH EU BUSINESS
INTEREST ASSOCIATIONS ARE CENTRAL

In this section, an attempt is made to briefly identify the significance of the
discussion about EU business interest associations to wider debates prevalent in
the academic literature; to introduce the practitioner reader to some of these
debates; and to signal for the academic reader some of the broader ideas in
which the data collection is embedded. These latter concepts will be developed
in the articulation of hypotheses that have guided the collection of data, and in
explaining the pattern of data collected (Chapter 3).

Many of the ideas presented in this book are wholly fresh contributions to the
study of EU business interest associations, drawn from a unique, large data-set
of 49 EU business associations and 151 of their members. Other ideas presented
adapt, or adopt, a rich heritage of literature in the study of business interest associations, often drawn from other settings. For instance, the most comprehensive
series of studies of business interest associations were those undertaken under
the umbrella of the Organisation of Business Interests (OBI) project undertaken
in the 1980s. This project brought together a collection of researchers to study
290 associations drawn from a range of sectors in nine countries, examining:

> whether and under what conditions business as a collective actor is able to
> organise itself into comprehensive, encompassing, hierarchically ordered,
> monopolistic organisations, capable of exercising control over their members,
> while at the same time representing their interests *vis-à-vis* other actors and in
> the polity. (Streeck and Schmitter, 1985; vii; see also the project research
> design in Streeck and Schmitter, 1981)

Thus, the research questions under investigation in the OBI project focused upon
some of the issues examined in this one. The analysis produced by the OBI
research network provides helpful tools and a wealth of literature with which to
approach this study, and this author acknowledges with gratefulness the intellectual legacy of this project. Nonetheless, this project is not an OBI mark II. Apart
from the differences in scope of the research questions, the principal distinctive-
ness of this study concerns its focus upon the EU level of organisation, whereas
the OBI project focused on national business interest associations. As has been
argued, the EU environment exerts its own distinctive impact upon business
associations. For instance, EU associations exist primarily for political representation purposes, whereas national associations provide their members with a full
range of member services. Thus, the average level of staffing of associations
studied in the OBI project was 66, whereas the available information for EU
associations suggests a comparable figure of less than one-tenth of these levels.

Indicators such as this suggest that EU associations are quite different animals from their national counterparts, requiring study in their own right. In addition, there is a wealth of literature since the OBI project from which to draw. These factors are in evidence throughout the book, and in the selection of introductory concepts presented below.

Business Interest Associations in European Integration

Whilst it is now *de rigeur* to seek hybrids amongst the many 'new' labels posing as theories of European integration, there remain in essence two main sources in which accounts are grounded. The first of these sees states in the pursuit of their interests as the principal source of integration. In consequence, the role played by 'outside interests' in civil society is seen as having peripheral significance, in that it is largely seen as confined to routine, technical policy areas, or as one of a number of contributory factors to domestic influences upon member state behaviour. In this account, the capacities of interest groups are therefore not a mainstream issue for enquiry. This perspective should be borne in mind, as it must be recognised that many significant EU policy outcomes such as (drawing from recent cases) Monetary Union, enlargement or electricity liberalisation cannot be explained by reference to actions by 'outside interests'. However, some policy outcomes can be, and it is in this second type of account, where most emphasis is placed upon the role of the institutions of the European Union, that the relationship between EU institutions, outside interests and member states is viewed as a central mechanism of European integration. The capacities of groups to act as dynamic agents of integration is therefore a substantial topic for investigation, and one to which this book is addressed.

In these latter 'institutionalist'-type accounts of European integration, emphasis is placed on the way in which outside interests such as firms and interest groups help to provide a constituency of demand for the transfer of competencies to the EU. Early, 'neo-functionalist' variants of institutionalism drew attention to the ways in which supranational institutions such as the European Commission worked together with interests in civil society, such as business, to seek common desired ends such as a single market and in consequence the expansion of European integration. The ways in which such interests worked on member states as a demand constituency for further European integration was termed by Haas (1958), the inventor of the neo functionalism concept, as 'political spillover'. The role of the European Round Table of Industrialists in creating the political support among member states for of the single market, encouraged by the European Commission, looks very much like an example of the 'political spillover' component of 'neo-functionalism'. Indeed, the European Commission has invested a good deal of effort and resources to nurturing and supporting interest groups on the basis that they will be invaluable allies in furthering European integration. Many citizen interest groups could not function without the financial support provided to them by the European Commission (sometimes using budget lines with uncertain legal application), or the wider patronage from the designated status provided to them by being given 'badges' such as an 'information observatory'. In turn, these have helped such interests identify with 'project Europe'. In addition to seeing such interests as allies in the quest for further European integration, such interests are seen as a way of providing these democratically-remote EU institutions with legitimacy, and a channel of communication to 'grassroots' concerns in the member states.

This emphasis upon 'political spillover' mechanisms of integration from early neo-functionalist accounts is helpfully updated by the varieties of 'new institutionalism'. Neo-functionalism went out of fashion during the 1960s and 1970s as states seemed to be in control of the process and progress of European integration, but its institutionalist foundations returned to popular status in the 1980s as actions by business interests (like the ERT) once again seemed to explain how European integration arose. 'New institutionalist' concepts added to our understanding by addressing the very pertinent question of how the behaviour, or even the very beliefs that interest groups hold, are shaped and constructed. At their most extended, 'new institutionalist' ideas draw from sociology in showing how the beliefs and values of interest groups derive from the influences that surround them, and in particular the institutional settings of the EU in which they participate. For those of us who frequently find ourselves internalising and repeating to others the wisdom we have picked up from the meetings we attend, this approach resonates with plausibility. More limited versions, however, dispute that interest groups' beliefs are constructed so significantly by their external environment, but draw attention to the ways in which interests respond to the stimuli provided by the rules, norms and conventions of the institutions they address in their behaviour. Hence, interest associations quickly find out what the rules are, and then play to the rules of the game.

In these accounts, the emphasis upon interest-group behaviour and even the construction of their belief systems as a response to the institutional settings in which they participate, contribute to our understanding of how the relationships between civil society interests and European institutions works as a mechanism of European integration. Because business interests remain the best mobilised of all 'outside interests', and, despite an increasing tendency in recent years for large firms to act outside of formal interest associations, such associations remain the mainstay of interaction between the EU institutions and business. The plausibility of accounts of European integration which are posited on the relationship between the EU institutions and outside interests are therefore dependent upon the ability of business interest associations organised at the European level to be 'up to the job'. That is, are EU business interest associations sufficiently cohesive and strong to be dynamic agents of European integration? If the answer to this question is 'no', this poses a major question for those accounts of the integration process founded upon the relationship between interest groups and the EU institutions.

Collective Action

'Collective action' has been a central debate to interest-group scholars since the work of Mancur Olson in 1965. Olson challenged the basis of interest-group analysis by questioning whether like-minded interests would automatically associate. Using principles derived from economics, Olson used the concept of rational pursuit of interests on the part of the potential member to show how membership would not arise if benefit could be derived without bearing the cost of membership. That is, it the benefit of interest-group activity could be obtained without joining, so the most logical behaviour would be to 'free-ride' the benefit. Free-riding would particularly arise in the political representation work of interest groups, in that any benefits negotiated with state authorities would apply universally (such as industry regulation or deregulation) rather than be restricted to interest-group members only. In consequence, Olson argued, interest groups would need to develop special incentives that were only accessible through membership.

This highly plausible analysis is somewhat problematic when applied to business interest associations at the EU level, because the principle purpose of most of these is political representation. At the national level, where business interest associations often provide a sophisticated range of services to members who may or may not be interested in political representation, Olson's account may have much to offer. But at the EU level, the issues are somewhat different. Mostly, members are already politically active and so do not require special incentives to encourage them to join their corresponding behaviour (Gray and Lowery, 1997). Hence, joining the association is simply normal political behaviour – 'the thing to do'. This particularly applies in the case of associations of national associations, whose members' existence partly derives from needs for political representation. It may also apply equally to large firms who accept that with size comes the responsibility to lead political action, and who regard association membership as normal political behaviour that does not require any special incentive.

Notwithstanding the above, a number of the 'goods' produced by associations which concentrate on political representation can be classified as 'incentives' in the Olsonian sense. An association with a strong reputation provides its own membership incentives. Getting one's own position endorsed under the collective badge of the association, or using the collective cloak of the association, is a strong membership incentive. Similarly, information produced by the association, or available from the network of other members of the association, is an incentive that can most easily be accessed by joining. So, too, are the activities and behaviour or the association, in that those not in membership lose the ability to influence these. Some members may not be able to identify a positive benefit they have obtained from their membership, but the *costs of non-membership* – such as the loss of access to the network, or the loss of ability to influence the positions of the membership (sometimes to prevent it from damaging the potential membership) – means that membership arises and prevails. All of these factors are in some way membership incentives. Quite different are the set of ideas that suggest that membership arises from 'habit', in following paths of behaviour that are taken as norms from the wider environment. These latter concepts, in which there is little resembling a calculated decision, are derived from sociology and social psychology and are distinct from the incentive-driven concepts provided by the economic notion of following a path of self-interest. Much of the data collection described later in this book is driven by the question as to whether associability at the EU level is incentive-driven. Apart from satisfying curiosity, this debate is somewhat central to the strategy formation of those who lead EU business associations.

The Nature and Structure of Business Interests in Political Systems

Many of the issues arising in the chapters that follow have their origins in debates initiated by Olson. His work on collective action can be extended to help explain a number of features surrounding the nature and structure of business interests in political systems. For instance, fragmentation and specialisation in the landscape of business interest organisation is a function of collective-action logics in which a calculus of interest has a central part to play. Thus, the rewards of one's participation, such as influence or a share of the lobbying victories obtained, is proportionately greater in small-membership associations because the chances of coherence and common agreement are greater in such associations. Beyond his work on collective action lies the more pejorative analysis of the role of special (largely, business) interest groups in retarding wealth creation and skewing its distribution by extracting special favours from governments as a result of their pressures and influences, and engaging in cartel-like behaviour. Crudely, Olson suggested that the performance of economies was inversely related to the presence and strength of special interest groups. Thus, the sluggish performance of the UK in the twentieth century was seen as a factor arising from the ability of embedded, specialised interest groups to extract special privileges from the state, and in doing so distorting the optimum efficiency of markets and disabling governance capacities. In Germany and Japan, on the other hand, the postwar destruction of the interest-group infrastructure alongside the rest of their economies enabled unhindered governance (Olson, 1971).

These conclusions are keenly contested, with other authors challenging the connection (for a review of these see Wilson, 1995) and pointing to the ability of associations to undertake functions in the broader public interest. Streeck and Schmitter show how associations can act as an intermediary between state and civil society as wider governance partners, organising and enforcing co-operative behaviour among their members, resolving conflicts, and acting as agents of implementation after seeking and obtaining delegated authority from states. Societies with 'associative capacities' are more capable of resolving questions of governability and avoiding market failure (Streeck and Schmitter, 1985). Doner and Schneider show how associations can act as agents of macroeconomic growth and inflation reduction through resolving classic dilemmas of collective action by enforcing industry-wide action, and can manage requirements for stability with needs for economic change and development (Doner and Schneider, 2001a). In order to undertake these functions, associations require a high degree of strength and internal capacities. These required properties are reviewed in Chapter 3, but foremost in their formation are the extent to which states provide patronage for associations.

States that can 'licence' associations and provide them with status as official interlocutors and governance partners endow such associations with strength and status as worthwhile organisations for potential members to be part of. In these contexts, associations become the principal feature of business–government relations, and are incorporated into governance systems. Historically, 'corporatist'-leaning systems common to the Germanic countries have followed this pattern, such that in 1938 nearly 50 per cent of Germany's industrial output was subject to price and production controls which were devised and managed by trade associations acting through the devolved authority of government (Schneiberg and Hollingsworth, 1991). In the more recent past, the Austrian model, with its compulsory membership of economic chambers, has been the model of economic management in which associations have featured most strongly. At the other extreme lie economic systems in which associations are just one part of a system of dialogue between business and government, with state–company dialogue frequently bypassing and undermining associations, and associations acting as just one type of actor among many as pluralist agents of 'pressure politics'. In these latter systems, such as those in Anglo-American societies, the state either refuses to patronise and licence an associational system, or lacks the capacity to do so. The EU with its fragmented architecture of power falls in this latter category, and in consequence EU associations do not form part of an overall system of governance.

In addition to multiple layers of power creating associational weakness by providing for multiple arenas for interest representation, the endemic fragmentation of power can also provide some insulation for political decision-making from private interests by EU institutions. This is a point developed most notably by Grande, building upon earlier work by Scharpf (1988) on the 'joint decision trap' common to federal systems. Grande notes how decision-making inputs include multiple institutional players with different perspectives, how bargains between private interests and institutional actors in EU decision-making can lack durability as the focus of decision-making moves to other arenas, and how the European Commission can sometimes skilfully play different interests off against one another in acting as a multilevel power broker (Grande, 1996). In these circumstances, the European Commission is able to insulate itself from pressures by outside interests, further eroding the vitality of associations. Whilst all EU business associations suffer from this general lack of patronage, there are nonetheless variations in the patronage of business associations by EU institutions that do go part way to explaining their differences in capacities and strength. These, and the location of other variations, are the causes of this book.

The foregoing analysis indicates the importance of institutions to economic performance, whether state institutions or business associations. Whilst Olson introduced economic principles to the analysis of political behaviour, his work is seen within economics as softening its classical assumptions because of its focus upon institutions as a variable in economic performance. Olson is one of the 'four gospels' of 'new institutional economics', whose work, along with that of Coase, North and Williamson, changed the course of economic analysis by challenging some of the foundations of classical economics. The common focus of 'new institutional economics' (NIE) is provided by institutions, and in doing so goes beyond the marketplace in seeking to show how government, the legal system, politics and interaction in groups are central contributory factors to wider economic performance.

Williamson placed special emphasis upon the 'transaction costs' of doing business in modern societies, covering most aspects other than the manufacture of a product leading up to the final sales transaction.[5] A high cost in transacting is that involved in measuring the value of what is being exchanged, which involves collecting information. In societies simpler than our own where transactions arose between known entities, trust provided a major means of assurance to transactions. This mechanism proved insufficient with the onset of complex societies, where transactions were typically impersonal and required an elaborate system of property rights to protect them. Monitoring and enforcing these rights are also costly, again because of the costs involved in information collection to ensure that ownership rights (the right to use, to derive income from the use of, the right to

---

[5] For Arrow, transaction costs can be defined more broadly as the 'costs of running the economic system' (Williamson, 1996).

exclude, and the right to exchange) prevail. It is this costliness that is the stimulus for economic and political behaviour, and the institutions that bound and regulate these. Williamson drew attention to the way in which such costs increased with the frequency of transactions, the specificity of the assets involved, and the uncertainty of contexts. These costs are the source of institutions in modern life (Williamson, 1996); although Williamson did not explicitly discuss the role of associations, they are one type of these instit utions involved in the regulation of transaction costs. Associations can offset the high costs of 'monitoring' for any one member by sharing it between them, providing a major motivation for collective action. That is, *associations can lower transaction costs*, either in managing and regulating markets themselves, or in seeking or responding to the regulation created by other institutions. Hollingsworth, Schmitter and Streeck argue that:

> In all modern economies, companies have associated with each other to collect information about production levels and prices, to conduct joint research and development, to promote standardization, to engage in technology transfer and vocational training, to channel communication and influence to state agencies, to formulate codes of conduct, to negotiate with labor, and even to decide on prices, production goals, and investment strategies. (1994: 7)

Yet the ability of associations to perform this range of functions, that is to manage markets by regulating competition within them, can be limited by the imposition of rules preventing them from doing so. Competition policy can place severe restrictions on the boundaries within which associations can operate, and their appeal to potential members. Because European Union competition policy is among the strictest of regimes to be found anywhere, so it restricts the scope of EU associations in comparison to the role of associations in other political systems. The utility of transaction-cost economics to the EU setting of business associations is further explored in Chapter 3.

Of all the 'four gospels' of new institutional economics, the 'softest' focus is provided by the work of North, with its emphasis upon the continuing role of trust in regulating transactions in modern societies by reducing uncertainties and thus the cost of acquiring information (North, 1990). Trust can be built up through repeated transactions between the same parties, or between parties colonising stable systems in which long-term relationships arise. If fragmentation produces distrust in markets, so too will it among associations and their members, and in systems such as the EU where business interest organisation is highly fragmented. Nonetheless, associations can reduce uncertainty by acting as agents of stability by structuring interaction and fostering trust, both between members, and with the other institutions they address whether economic (such as other types of business in the product chain) or political institutions

(Chapter 3). Similarly, associations can work well in conditions of high trust between members, and between the secretariat and members. These trust conditions can be a product of the environment in which members operate, such as a limited number of firms operating together in international marketplaces under similar conditions. Trust can also be stimulated, such as through social exchanges between trade association members and the secretariat. Where conditions of high trust arise, so too will the shared understandings, and the autonomy of a secretariat to create these, on which coherent associations thrive. Consequently, the chapters ahead devote considerable analysis to the contribution that trust and associational autonomy can make to associational capacities, and the ways in which these arise and can be developed. In the chapters ahead, these are considered alongside a systematic evaluation of each of the other factors that might be held to influence the capacities of EU business associations, whether in the institutional environment (markets and politics), or the organisational and management actions that impact upon associations.

2 Methodology

The data-set upon which this research is based is unique. Interviews were undertaken with 49 EU business associations, and 151 of their members and non-members, making it easily the most comprehensive analysis of EU business associations ever undertaken. Yet 'interest-group' type research is notoriously weak and unreflective on methods, despite (and perhaps because of) the complexity of the topics being investigated. This complexity derives from the relational nature of most of the topics under investigation, such as the impact of a particular private interest source upon a public policy outcome, or the factors at play between an association and its members, or between its members. Because the conclusions drawn from an analysis are only as good as the methodology employed, this chapter identifies the approaches used, articulates the rationale informing the choices made, traces the steps undertaken in collecting the data, and discusses the issues that arose as the data were collected. In laying these out, the aim is to ensure that the reader can:

- understand how, and why, the author has been able to reach the conclusions reported in Chapters 4–6;
- trace the steps taken by the author in arriving at these; and
- reach an independent judgement of confidence in the conclusions and analysis presented.

DEDUCTIVE OR INDUCTIVE METHODOLOGIES?

Chapter 1 identified the reasons for undertaking an analysis of EU business associations, reasons which justify their study as an enquiry in its own right, and as a means of contributing to wider debates. These debates include those on the dynamics of integration, of collective action, and the role and power of business in governance. These contexts and debates within which EU associations are embedded provide a series of issues which structure the analysis, and which can be translated as a series of research questions to investigate. In methodological terms, these research questions are generated *deductively* from logical reasoning, usually prompted by the wider literature. To these can be added questions that arise as a result of *inductive* investigation, either through *experiences*, or from exploring issues *interactively*, with the focus of enquiry, here EU business associations. Inductive research therefore involves identifying research questions and issues from the process of data collection with the subject of enquiry itself.

In practice, most research is a mixture of both, particularly if the researcher has been an investigator in the field for some time, with knowledge (in this instance) of EU business associations derived from previous investigations and networks of practitioners working in and with such associations. After researching a phenomenon for some time, it becomes difficult in practice to distinguish the origin of knowledge as inductive or deductive. Nonetheless, the distinction is worth making, because analysis based on deductive reasoning requires validation or challenge by the reality of practice, whereas the reality of practice involves interpretation that draws upon deductive reasoning. On its own, deductive reasoning, no matter how well conceived, can be mere speculation or prediction. Frequently, it misses insights that are only likely to come from in-depth investigation of practice, or that which can be yielded by practitioners. Deductive research can focus the researcher's attention too narrowly, in that he or she is likely to find confirmatory evidence of what is being looked for, and miss other issues which might have been suggested by an initial survey of experiences on the ground. Inductive research, on the other hand, runs the risk of missing the big picture, of being insufficiently focused, of leading to blind alleys, and to conclusions borne of a variety of data collection errors. Among the latter, those originating from small sample size, failure to reach the right contact, or overdependence upon particular sources, can be typical difficulties for research of this type. Whilst it is difficult to distinguish between the origin of knowledge as deductive or inductive, it is possible to deliberately seek to incorporate each concept in a research design, systematically investigating hypotheses (deductive), and using hypotheses as a synthesis in itself (inductive).

The aim of the research was to identify, assess and weigh factors which help explain variation in the governability of EU business associations, that is their ability to unify their members' interests and to ensure compliance among members with associational aims. Chapter 3 identifies the 28 factors of investigation, together with a rationale for their selection and weighting. Each of these *processes* – factor identification, weighting and assessment – was derived from a mixture of inductive yield and deductive reasoning, although the balance of deductive and inductive origins differs for each of these processes. It also differed by the stage of the research. Interviews with the 49 EU business associations were conducted first (stage 1), followed by the member/non-member interviews (stage 2). This allowed issues raised inductively with EU associations in the first stage to guide the construction of questions to be explored with members in the second stage. Thus,

- *Identification* of factors for research among the EU associations were drawn from deductive reasoning and from inductive experiences, or a mixture of each of these. As is described in Chapter 3, there is a literature on associational governability drawn from comparative politics which provided 'signposts' for data collection. These signposts were customised to the EU context, and added to by the author's research and network experiences with EU business associations.[1] For research among members, the factors raised inductively through the research conducted among EU associations was mixed with deductive reasoning to guide data collection.

- *Weighting* of the 28 factors was undertaken by a mixture of deductive reasoning and experiential and interactive inductive data collection, undertaken among EU associations and with members. A scale of 1 (lowest impact) to 5 (highest impact) was used to express a generally applicable weighting for each factor.

- *Assessment* of each EU business association against each factor was undertaken exclusively by inductive data collection, drawn from multiple sources of evidence, including, for each case, an interview from sources connected with the EU association and its members (and sometimes a non-member) together with a range of literature provided by the association. Each association was weighted against the factor concerned on a scale 1 (low) to 5 (high), and then multiplied against the factor weighting. In this way, a particular association emerged with a 'governability' score, with two 'league tables' constructed from a simple assessment and a weighted assessment. As described in Chapter 4, these produced similar placings in the table. Associations were then assessed comparatively with others in the rank orderings in order to identify factors in common, thus helping to identify both the causal factors of variation, the factors in combination, and their relative importance.

The guiding methodological source – deductive or inductive – are identified for both stages of data collection, for each of the research processes undertaken, in Table 2.1.

Table 2.1 Methodological source of data collection by research process and stage

Research process	Stage 1: EU business associations	Stage 2: members/ non-members
Factor identification	Deductive and inductive experience	Deductive and inductive interaction
Weighting	Deductive and inductive experience and interaction	Deductive and inductive experience and interaction
Assessment	Inductive interaction	Inductive interaction

[1] See, for instance, Greenwood Grote and Ronit (1992), Greenwood (1995), Greenwood (1997), Greenwood and Aspinwall (1998), and Compston and Greenwood (2001).

DATA COLLECTION

The type of information required to satisfy these needs, and to satisfy the information required from each association against the factors identified in Chapter 3, was essentially qualitative, with some requirements for expressing the data analysed in a quantitative way.[2] Given the greater emphasis upon inductive interactive data in the first stage, interview design demanded a focused, unstructured approach. As this approach helped guide the data collection in the second stage, a focused and structured approach to data collection was then taken with an interview questionnaire. This is reproduced in Appendix 1.[3]

EU Business Associations

The EU associations chosen for analysis were based on a number of criteria. The first of these was to undertake research among business-wide associations, a relatively easy task in that it involved undertaking interviews with all five organisations in this category. A second criteria was to undertake research among 'sectoral', or specific business associations. These were too numerous (Chapter 1) for in-depth analysis of the entire population, and consequently required some form of sampling. The principal factor of differentiation from which to select a sample was associational format, following the proportions for the universe of EU business associations specified in Chapter 1. Thus, 57 per cent of this sample would be associations of associations, 18 per cent would be direct membership, and 25 per cent would be mixed. Balancing the requirements for reasonable sample sizes to match these proportions against the available resources of time and funding (2 months in Brussels), produced the total of approximately 50 associations to investigate, or a sample representing a little over 5 per cent of the universe of EU business associations. Beyond this, differentiation was sought so as to achieve representation of sub-sectoral, sectoral and cross-sectoral associations, and a variety of factors presented following the discussion below.

A decision was taken to restrict interviews to Brussels-based associations on a number of grounds. It is recognised that these constitute a shade under

---

[2] 'Interval' data lies along a hierarchy of categories of data, from 'nominal' to 'ratio'. 'Nominal' identifies categories where no hierarchy is intended, such as by colour. 'Ordinal' specifies a hierarchy of categories, such as 'large', 'medium' and 'small'. Interval data specifies the differentiation between the hierarchies with specific values assigned into categories.

[3] During the course of data collection, minor alterations to the original interview questionnaire for members of EU business associations were undertaken, aimed at rephrasing questions or adding questions to explore similar issues, rather than adding new factors. These minor changes did not affect assessment of the EU association against the factors examined. The version appearing in Appendix 1 is the most recent version of the two used.

two-thirds of all EU business associations (Chapter 1) and skew the sample profile towards the better-resourced associations from larger sectors. For this very reason it was anticipated that access to interview respondents would be easier, because Brussels-based associations are more likely to have a permanent secretariat and premises. Thus, an approach would be made to a full-time salaried official with a thorough knowledge of the workings of the association, working in a dedicated organisation with supporting office facilities where contact could be made. The alternative scenario might involve seeking out lay board members from an unstaffed, or semi-staffed, organisation, working in scattered locations with variable roles and experiences in, and knowledge of and time for, an association. An approach to the former category was also thought to offer uniformity through interviewing respondents in a similar position. The need to efficiently use available resources was also a consideration in order to maximise the number of interviews that could be undertaken. This factor was also important at a time when just one researcher (the author) was undertaking the research interviews in order to uniformly implement a research design that was partly dependent upon inductively identifying factors for investigation.

Following data collection among EU business associations, a phase of interviews with their members and non-members was planned, with the numbers of these to be undertaken determined by the availability of resources. In the event, funding was located so as to undertake approximately 150 member/non-member interviews, representing an average of three per association, varied by size so that the largest EU associations would be subject to more member interviews, and vice versa. These considerations yielded the numbers of interviews with different types of EU associations in stage 1, shown in Table 2.2.

Choice of the specific EU business associations to approach within these categories was taken on a number of criteria, based upon deductive differentiation drawn from the literature reported in Chapter 3, and from inductive experience.

Table 2.2 Associational format of EU associations sampled

Category	Number of interviews	% of all interviews	% of interviews from domain-based[*] associations
Associations of associations	25	52	58
Direct firm membership	8	16	16
Mixed	11	22	26
Cross-sectoral	5	10	

[*] That is, not business-wide associations.

The subjectivity and difficulties presented by measurement of a number of these factors, itemised below, meant that information on them was drawn by approximations taken from a number of sources. These included directories of associations, and advice from consultations with a number of sources from the Brussels world of business and public affairs. Associations throughout the scale of most of the factors below were selected, according to:

- size, both of the economic interest represented and the association secretariat, using data from Butt Philip and Gray (1996) and Euroconfidentiel (1998);
- type, ranging from manufacturing to service, using directory sources such as Landmarks (1998);
- levels of industry concentration, together with distributions of firm size;
- sector stability, including significant merger and acquisition activities;
- geographical basis of markets;
- different stages of the product cycle;
- interests at different stages of the product chain, from primary, to processing, to market;
- degree of specialisation;
- stability and change of leadership;
- degree and type of regulation;
- the presence or absence of

  - 'high politics' issues in the domain, and the extent to which an interest was contested by organised public interests; or
  - self-regulation.

In addition, some assessment was taken as to likeliness of access to the particular association in question. Indeed, access to the target group of interviewees – the Chief Executive Officer/General Secretary of each of these organisations proved relatively unproblematic, with just two refusals to participate.[4] In most cases, the interview was granted enthusiastically, with considerable interest expressed in the potential research findings. In a small number of cases, a substitute for the General Secretary was designated, usually as a result of unforeseen events at the time of the appointment. All of these interviews were conducted in October and November 1998 by the author. These criteria taken into account, this 5.2 per cent sample of EU business associations appears to provide a reasonable basis upon which to draw conclusions about the population of EU business associations as a whole, although it is not claimed, for the reasons outlined above, that the degree of representivity is similar to that which would have arisen from an entirely random sample.

---

[4] Two associations – 1 medium and 1 small – felt unable to participate through lack of time. These organisations were subsequently replaced by others similar in format and size.

Members of EU Business Associations

The number of member interviews undertaken was determined by a variety of factors. On resource grounds, a ceiling of approximately 150 member/non-member interviews was imposed. These were distributed between EU business associations primarily on the grounds of an approximation of size of domain represented, although this was moderated by considerations of national distribution and the logistics of travel and available resources. Efforts were also concentrated, though not exclusively, upon conducting member interviews for sectoral, or domain, associations, rather than in respect of those associations seeking to represent business-wide interests. This was because the principal aim of the research focused upon variation in governability, the need to compare factors across associations, the small number of business-wide associations and the presence of alternative sources of information about cross-business associations. These alternative sources included the EU sectoral associations, and members of sectoral associations. Many of these held established links, including in some cases membership, of cross-business associations, and were able to offer informed insights. There was a case for removing the cross-business associations completely from the analysis, in that they are quite different in scope, function and dynamics than are domain-based associations. On balance, more of the 28 factors were applicable to them than were not, and in consequence they were kept in and rated against a much more restricted set of factors than were domain-based associations. Discussion of them is, however, kept separate, with Chapter 5 devoted to cross-sectoral associations whereas the results from domain-specific associations are presented in Chapter 4. They are included in the table at the end of this chapter, presenting a summary of the interviews undertaken.

The 151 member interviews were conducted between January 1999 and May 2001 by a team of 12 researchers, including 6 different native language speakers, although almost half of all member interviews were conducted by the author.[5] Funding to undertake these interviews was obtained from 12 separate sources, with no one source providing more than 20 per cent of the amount required. Members were chosen in order to achieve a balanced sample by geographical location, and where possible by size of member, and were generally undertaken on the same trip to a particular country.[6] These criteria yielded an interview sample of 103 national associations (68%), 2 EU associations, and 46 companies

---

[5] Language did not present a barrier because it is a requirement for the person managing the relationship with the EU association to be able to converse fluently in either (and increasingly; see Guéguen, 2001) English or French.
[6] With the exception of Belgium, where large companies with public affairs offices there were interviewed during the course of a number of trips.

Table 2.3 National composition of sample of
national association members and non-member
associations of EU business associations

Austria	2
Belgium	5
Denmark	5
Finland	2
France	13
Germany	18
Greece	3
Hungary	3
Ireland	3
Italy	6
Netherlands	6
Norway	2
Portugal	2
Spain	5
Sweden	3
UK	25
Total	103

(32%).[7] This composition is approximately equal to the proportion of EU associations that are associations of associations (57%), and of companies (19%), plus an equal share of the 25 per cent of EU associations that are mixed in composition between companies and national associations. No attempt was made to classify a national breakdown of companies, given that the large companies who are direct members of EU associations are frequently multinationals. Table 2.3 provides a national breakdown of the national association members interviewed.

There are no figures available for the actual numbers of associations from these countries affiliated to EU associations. Were they to be so, these would yield a different breakdown from those in Table 2.3, although there is an approximation of large, medium and small countries from the figures presented in Table 2.3. There is nothing in the profile of associations represented in this table to suggest that the results presented in Chapter 4 would have been radically different if proportionately more associations from smaller countries, and less from larger countries, had been included in the sample. Returns from interviews appeared to yield few 'nationally specific' characteristics that are central factors in the analysis of member behaviour in EU associations. One exception to this is a general trend for interests from countries with corporatist traditions (mainly, countries with Germanic-based languages) to place more emphasis upon the

---

[7] This number includes one national bank.

importance of their EU association (Boléat, 1996) than do those from countries with pluralist traditions. However, this difference is more pronounced in the case of company behaviour (Coen, 1997) than it is with national associations, the subject of Table 2.3.

In constituency-wide figures, associations from the UK, Germany and France would be, as in Table 2.3, the most represented in the sample, although proportionately less so than in Table 2.3, particularly in the case of the UK, and this should be borne in mind when interpreting the results presented in Chapter 4. So, too, should the point that a number of the other countries would be proportionately better represented, and there might be a wider representation of those from outside of western Europe. However, the representation of 16 countries from this latter category in the sample is presented as a strength, particularly given the logistical issues, including those of resourcing, of undertaking the requisite number of interviews in each of the different locations. It remains the case that the results presented in this book originate from the most comprehensive research on EU associations yet undertaken.

The target respondent in each of these national association members was the person responsible for managing their relationship with the EU business association. In the vast majority of cases, access was obtained to the target person in the target organisation with occasional use of substitutes where circumstances dictated. More problematic in concept was obtaining access to the person in large companies responsible for managing their affiliation to the EU association in question. Companies participate at a number of levels in EU associations, from strategic to technical. In large companies, and particularly those with decentralised cultures, it is often difficult to locate an individual with overall responsibility for managing the association. Associational membership may primarily 'belong' to, or originate from, a specialist division of a company. This difficulty is compounded where a company is multi-product, with a dense network of subsidiaries, and where the company and division has been subjected to considerable change influences. Those who took the original decision to affiliate to an association may well have moved on, and responsibility may have passed on, perhaps to a centralised public affairs division, for managing the relationship with the association. In other cases, a division may have been sold to a company with a quite different culture, and where there is more centralised coordination of public affairs. As reported in Chapter 4, these circumstances have sometimes led to conflicts between a division used to a decentralised culture and managing its own public affairs, and the new company with a more centralised tradition, and the division resists any attempts at control. Because no clear trends were evident from the start of the research, other than for responsibilities to be shared for managing the EU association, a decision was made to interview the EU public affairs manager for the firm concerned. This decision was also partly taken on resource grounds.[8] In every case, the individual concerned was able to speak authoritatively about the EU association in question, and about their company affiliation to it, although very specific details such as the size of the affiliation fee were often unknown (see the discussion in Chapter 4 on the wider implications of this point). Once again, there was a negligible level of refusals once contact had been established with the individual concerned, with access facilitated by considerable interest throughout the interview sample in obtaining a summary of the results. In four cases, a telephone interview substituted for a face-to-face interview.

Confidentiality and Presentation of Results

Access throughout the study – whether to EU business associations or their members – may also have been facilitated by a general assurance of confidentiality that the results would not be presented in a way that could identify the respondent. The integrity of this assurance has been treated as absolute and with the utmost priority throughout the presentation of results in this book. The intention was never to write detailed case descriptions of individual associations and the relationships with their members, but to locate the most important factors responsible for variations in the governability of EU associations by comparing across associations. In Table 2.4, the names of the EU associations interviewed are identified, though the identities of members are not. This balance has been struck for several reasons.

Firstly, this is research placed in the public domain, and the reader needs to have some confidence in the results presented, and, in the pursuit of truth, rigour and discourse, to raise questions that require answers or which might qualify the interpretation of results. Secondly, the research is aimed at identifying the causal factors of variation. Each association is assessed against each of the 28 factors hypothesised to cause variation, and those findings have to be presented and discussed by comparing common factors across associations if the aim of the research is to be realised. Thirdly, there is no convenient shorthand that could be used to clearly present results, particularly as a number of factors are concerned with characteristics of domains or sectors, and product markets. It would be neither plausible nor sufficiently clear, for instance, to present the findings from 'an association representing a specialist segment of the transport sector', while in other domains the identity of associations would be so obvious to readers that any disguise would be a thin pretence.

Member identities are not revealed because the presentation of results does not require it. The focus of the enquiry is variation in the governability of EU

---

[8] Such individuals are concentrated on locations in Brussels.

Table 2.4 EU business associations, members and non-members interviewed

Association	Format* (dfm = direct firm membership, f = federation; m = mixed; x = cross-sectoral and issue)	Member
ACE Alliance for Beverage Cartons and the Environment	dfm	1 company 1 non-member company
ACEA European Automobile Manufacturers Association	dfm	5 companies
AEA Association of European Airlines	dfm	4 companies
AIM European Brands Association	m	1 company 1 national association 1 EU association
AMCHAM-EU The EU Committee of the American Chamber of Commerce	x	2 companies
CAOBISCO Association of the Chocolate Biscuit and Confectionary Industries of the EU	f	4 national associations
CBMC Brewers of Europe	f	3 national associations 1 non-member company
CEA European Insurance Committee	f	6 national associations
CEFIC European Chemical Industry Council	m	4 national associations 3 companies
CEMBUREAU The European Cement Association	f	2 national associations
CEPS European Confederation of Spirits Producers	f	2 national associations
CIAA Confederation of the Food and Drink Industries of the EU	f	5 national associations
CIMSCEE Committee of the Mustard Industries in the European Economic Community	f	
COCERAL Committee of Cereals, Oilseeds, Animal Feed, Olive Oil, Oils & Fats & Agrosupply Trade in the EU	f	3 national associations

Table 2.4   Continued

Association	Format*(dfm = direct firm membership; f = federation; m = mixed; x = cross-sectoral and issue)	Member
COLIPA European Cosmetic Toiletry & Perfumery Association	m	2 national associations
COPA/COGECA Committee of Agricultural Organisations in the EU	f	4 national associations 1 EU association
CPIV Standing Committee of the European Glass Industries	f	1 national association
EAAA European Advertising Agencies	m	2 national associations
EACEM European Association of Consumer Electronics Manufacturers	m	3 companies
EAT European Advertising Tripartite	m	1 company
EBU European Banking Union	f	3 national associations 1 non-member company 1 national bank
EBU European Broadcasting Union	m	3 national associations 1 company
ECA European Carpet Association	f	1 national association
ECF European Coffee Federation	m	2 national associations
ECSA European Community Shipowners Association	f	2 national associations
EDA European Dairy Association	f	4 national associations
EEO European Express Organisation	dfm	1 company 1 non-member company
EFA European Driving Schools Association	f	2 national associations
EFCA European Federation of Consulting Engineers	f	4 national associations
EFPIA European Federation of Pharmaceutical Industry Associations	m	2 national associations 1 company

Table 2.4 Continued

Association	Format* (dfm = direct firm membership; f = federation; m = mixed; x = cross-sectoral and issue)	Member
EGTA European Group of Television Advertisers	dfm	2 companies
EMOTA European Mail Order Traders Association	f	3 national associations
ERT European Round Table of Industrialists	x	1 company
ETRTO European Tyre and Rim Technical Organisation	f	2 non-member companies
EURATEX European Apparel and Textile Organisation	f	3 national associations
EURELECTRIC Union of the Electricity Industry	f	4 national associations 2 companies[**]
EUROCHAMBRES Association of European Chambers of Commerce & Industry	x	5 national associations
EUROCHLOR European Chlorine Association	dfm	2 companies
EUROCOMMERCE European Federation of Retailing and Distribution	f	3 national associations 1 associate company member
EUROFER European Confederation of Iron and Steel Industries	m	4 national associations
EUROPABIO European Association for Bioindustries	m	1 company
EUROPIA/CONCAWE European Petroleum Industry Association/The Oil Companies' European Organisation for Environmental and Health Protection	dfm	5 companies
EUROPE'S 500	x	2 companies
EUROPECHE Association of National Organisations of Fishing Enterprises in the EU	f	3 national associations
FAEP European Federation of Magazine Publishers	f	2 national associations 1 non-member association

Table 2.4   Continued

Association	Format* (dfm = direct firm membership; f = federation; m = mixed; x = cross-sectoral and issue)	Member
FIEC European Construction Industry Federation	f	2 national associations 1 non-member national association
ORGALIME Liaison Group of the Mechanical, Electrical, Electronic and Metalworking Industries	f	3 national associations 1 non-member association
UEAPME European Association of Craft, Small & Medium-Sized Enterprises	x	2 national associations
UNICE Union of Industrial and Employers' Confederations of Europe	x	4 national confederations

* Classified at the time of interview. It is acknowledged that a small number of those associations interviewed have changed their format since.
** Company members are admitted where there is no national association as a result of a near monolith supplier.

business associations, and the specific identity of their members is therefore not required. Given the relatively low numbers of interviews conducted with some associational membership constituencies, it might also be sensitive for the relationships between associations and their members to reveal these identities. The information given about member interviews conducted in Table 2.4 is therefore restricted to summary numbers of associations and firms, and deviations from the norm such as the inclusion of a non-member, an EU association or an organisation outside the private sector. It had been the intention to include more 'non-members' among the interviews undertaken, but this proved problematic. Firstly, as explained in Chapter 4, non-members are very much the exception and are few and far between. Secondly, and consequently, the interviews that were undertaken with EU associations suggested that, where it had arisen, non-membership usually reflected highly purposeful, rather than 'by-default', behaviour. Examples include the wishes of a self-styled and highly individualistic entrepreneur (such as Cristal d'Arques in the glass industry); or a wish to remain apart from established operators for commercial positioning to maintain a crusading, mould-breaking change-agent image (such as Virgin in the airline industry).

It may also indicate a historic and specific dispute between the member and the association, sometimes from the legacy of bitter personality disputes, of which a small number of examples arose. All of these reasons yield sensitivities, and some suspicions about outsiders making contact wishing to undertake public-domain research on relatively isolated cases. Consequently, the non-member interviews were restricted to 10 (and 1 associate member), and five of these were ineligible for membership as a result of the format (e.g. association of associations) of the association in question. These five organisations, nonetheless, each had a direct and specific trading interest in the sector represented by the association, and were in a unique position to offer insights about the association concerned. Table 2.4 identifies and classifies all the interviews undertaken.

Data Quality

The high level of access secured through the interviews with EU association managers, national association officials responsible for managing the relationship with the EU association, and the Brussels-based public affairs managers of large firms provides one dimension of quality assurance. Another concerns the multiple sources of evidence, using a range of primary and secondary sources ranging across EU associations and their members (and in some cases non-members). Chapter 3 identifies the 28 factors of governability that were identified and assessed through the research, using the methods described in this chapter. Assessment of each of the factors concerned arose through most of the multiple sources of evidence described. In the majority of cases, information to assess these factors was unproblematic. Questions in primary data collection to do this ranged from the factual to the perceptual, and in most cases related directly to the factors under investigation. In some cases, assessment of the factors relied more upon the perceptions of the respondents than from external data, such as the degree of concentration of a sector, and the levels of merger and acquisitions activities. The two concepts that were not the subject of direct questions concern those of the autonomy of the association, and trust between members. Rather, assessment of these factors was explored in more subtle ways, indirectly, during the interview, though no less comprehensively or systematically. Some of the questions alluded to these concepts, and in some form always prompted the respondent to raise the subject directly. Many were anxious to air the subject openly as part of a wider interest in the topic under investigation, governability. Some had in mind a set of problems or issues that had arisen in the association, and found it helpful to articulate them. Almost all were interested to know the results arising from the study, and how a particular association compared to others.

In summary, the research process was a mixture of deductive and inductive processes. The choice of associations to focus on was based upon criteria drawn from deductive analysis, such as degree of specialism, and inductive experiences such as the impact of large firms upon collective action. These factors were assessed through inductive interaction by interviews with EU business associations, which helped reveal the relative importance of factors such as the impact of a 'common enemy'. Inductive interaction also yielded further factors for investigation among members, such as the extent of common identity between members provided by a 'European' identity in world trade regulation, and questioned some of the issues raised deductively from the literature such as the impact of competition on associability. Each association was then assessed against these factors through interviews with both the associations themselves, with their members, and in a small number of cases with their non-members, through a mixture of simple and weighted assessment. The weightings themselves were further refined by the round of member interviews. Finally, the process yielded a 'league table' of associational governability, enabling the comparison of associations clustered together in order to identify factors of commonality. These results are presented in Chapter 4, ahead of a review of the deductive factors drawn from the literature and presented in Chapter 3. Whilst there is a danger that this iterative, interactive relationship between deduction and induction ends as a self-fulfilling prophecy of validating the factors originally estimated as important, the process does raise new factors, challenges original assumptions, and produces clusters of comparable cases to identify common factors. The alternatives are unpalatable. Straightforward deduction can be little more than speculation, divorced from reality. Pure induction involves the pretence of 'disowning' prior knowledge, and runs the risk of reinventing the wheel by raising issues already well-established in the literature.

3 Governability Factors in EU Business Associations

In this chapter, the choice of each of the 28 factors held to differentiate associational governability are justified by reference to both previous research and analysis, and to factors which have arisen inductively following the data collection. In the case of the former, the established literature on associations requires some adaptation to the EU context. An explanation of each factor in the context of EU associations is followed in each case by a justification for their weighting and ranking which is used to provide the results presented in Chapter 4.

FACTOR 1: DEGREE OF SPECIALISM IN THE PRODUCT CHAIN

Specialism is endemic to business interest organisation, particularly in pluralist systems where associations are not 'licensed' by state authority (for a comprehensive literature review, see Bennett, 1998). The greater the decentralisation and dispersion of political power, the greater is the incentive for the formation of many voluntary associations (Wilson, 1995). The EU is in precisely this situation.

Whilst the 'logic of influence' described in Chapter 1 demands encompassingness, the 'logic of membership' described there also demands a narrow membership constituency from which cohesion can be drawn. In Olsonian cost/benefit terms, small-number associations increase the rewards of one's participation, such as influence or a share of the lobbying victories obtained (Olson, 1965). Specialism enables associations to define their membership boundaries, and assist an organisation to monopolise its boundary, that is to exist without having to compete with other associations for members. It also eases the task of finding common positions between members, because the constituent interests have a high degree of similarity. In Chapter 1, it was noted how associations are highly responsive to the stimuli of the state. These responses include the scope and complexity of regulatory policies by organising into specialisms that reflect regulatory organisation, and the impact of regulation. Consequently, the landscape of business interest associations is fragmented around these specialisms, unless governmental authority has sought a wider role for associations that requires a more encompassing breadth of membership. As was discussed in Chapter 1, the fragmented EU political system does not possess the 'stateness' to 'licence' associations in this way. Broad, encompassing associations can only work in a system of corporatist interest intermediation, where their breadth and detachment from any one specialised interest makes them valuable partners to governmental machinery, capable of simplifying consultative life and performing wider public interest services.

Whilst 'special interests' can be damaging to economic and political systems in the ways described by Olson (Chapter 1), the flip side is that they do advance the specialist interests they represent. The narrow specialisms typical of more pluralist systems like the EU can be organised around stages in the product chain, or around specialist manufacturing processes and product markets, or around issues and concepts (considered separately below). In the first of these, producers of raw materials (e.g. cocoa beans) and those who convert them into a product (e.g. chocolate) may have similar interests in ensuring a stable supply of the commodity, but they each have vastly different interests in the conditions governing the transactions of these products (e.g. prices). It is therefore easier for these competing interests to organise into separate associations where common agreement is likely to be possible, than it is for them to organise across the product chain. Similarly, it may be easier to organise specialist segments of production than to organise across specialisms. One example of this involves the number of EU associations in the glass industry, with separate organisations representing the interests of those who produce: flat glass; cut glass; container glass; technical glass; optical glass; television glass; glass fibres (insulation); and glass fibres (textiles).

Whilst such specialisms may make business interest organisation more cohesive and rewarding for those who participate in them, the resulting pattern of fragmentation may intensify competition between business interests, reducing both the overall influence of business in public policy outcomes, and for governments seeking a simplified consultative life. The latter desire has prompted a number of initiatives at member-state government level seeking to consolidate the number of representative associations into a handful of lead associations,[1] but these initiatives have not reversed the tide of a proliferation of associations. A further negative consequence of such specialisation is that associations may suffer from low levels of resourcing, which in turn may restrict the autonomy of an association and enhance its dependence upon members (Bennett, 1997a).

Streeck and Schmitter noted these conflicting tendencies; that is, between a 'logic of membership' encouraging specialisation in collective structures, and the 'logic of influence' towards larger size because of the demands of state agencies. These conflicting forces have found variable responses from business associations. EuroCommerce is an example of an EU association that has responded more to the 'logic of influence', with a significant level of staffing to service its

---

[1] In the UK, such initiatives included the 1972 Devlin Report, and the 'Heseltine initiatives' of 1993–95 (for a review see Bennett, 1997a).

wide interests. However, its breadth in organising across interests in the product chain (retail, wholesale, distribution, and even some manufacturing interests) makes it highly prone to lowest common denominator positions. In trading off between the conflicting logics of influence and membership, interests that prize collective cohesion most will invariably develop towards the logic of membership trajectory. The literature is almost unanimous in the view that without specialisation, associational cohesiveness is virtually impossible to achieve (Hayward, 1975; Streeck and Schmitter, 1981; Coleman, 1988; van Waarden, 1991; Wilson, 1995; Bennett, 1998).

Factor 1:   A high degree of specialism in a pluralist system enhances the ability of the association to unify its members' interests, whereas a low degree of specialism contributes to classic 'lowest common denominator' problems in reaching common positions. A high degree of specialism will also enable an association to avoid competing with other associations for members. Because of the strong association in the literature of specialisation with associational cohesiveness, this factor was given the top rating of '5'.

FACTOR 2: 'ISSUE-NICHE' ORGANISATIONS

A higher degree of specialisation still concerns 'issue niches', where an association does not seek to articulate views across a wide range of concerns but instead seeks to specialise on selected, narrow issues. At the European level, AIM, the European Brands Association, is one example of an issue-niche organisation, uniting manufacturers across sectors to protect the interests of branded products. Typically, these issues might involve those surrounding intellectual property protection, and the purchasing power of large retail chains. Another 'issue-niche' organisation is ACE, the Alliance for Beverage Cartons and the Environment, which addresses the environmental issues confronting carton manufacturers. This latter organisation searched for and found an agenda after its original purpose – to respond to a crisis health 'scare' – had receded.

Apart from describing the colonisation of specialist niches by associations, the literature draws attention to how associations monopolise the organisation and representation of a highly specialised interest niche through tacit agreement with other associations. Associations can thus acquire a reputation for specialising in a particular issue, and associations with otherwise potentially similar interest constituencies can avoid competing for members. This work is most closely associated with the work of Browne, who argues that:

An organised interest, in effect, gains a recognizable identity by defining highly specific issue niches for itself and fixing its activities within that niche ... various organised interests within a policy domain accommodate one another, usually by focusing on their own increasingly narrow demands. (Browne, 1990: 502)

Browne's work is seminal and rigorous, based on a two-year internship with an interest group. A high degree of specialism and mutual co-operation between associations is seen in his work as a means of coping with resource deficiencies, enabling each organisation to be most active in its own area of specialisation and to exchange the products of specialisation with others where necessary (Browne, 1977). Similarly, Schmitter argues that:

associations may appear to have defined their domains in ways that imply competition while in practice coming to less obtrusive arrangements under which they agree not to try to lure away each other's members or to share key resources and even leaders or to engage in a subtle division of labour *vis-à-vis* potential interlocutors. (Schmitter, 1992: 441)

Chapter 1 provided an example of a number of highly specialised EU associations in the processed food sector that appear to fit this description.

Factor 2:   The specialism of issue-niche organisation is highly associated with cohesiveness, though the high degree of specialism provides for a very narrow focus and a relatively small population of organisations, justifying a weighting factor of '3'.

FACTOR 3: MEMBERSHIP DENSITY

Every analysis of associations includes an assessment of the extent to which an association includes all potential members within its constituency domain, or its membership density. Those with a high degree of membership density do better, in that they are perceived to be authoritative and 'the organisation to be a part of'. Measurement of this factor is considerably easier in the case of associations of associations than with those that include firms. In both cases some relaxation of expectations is appropriate because of their status as EU-wide associations. It is not uncommon for confederate structures to be without a member from Luxembourg, or for at least one member from Greece, Portugal and Ireland. Associations that admit firms usually only seek to represent the large players, and there is little expectation that they can realistically expect to recruit small firms directly on a Europe-wide basis.

Factor 3:   A high degree of density is associated with organisational strength, and the status which derives from this adds to (though does not determine) cohesion. The indirectness of this concept, together with the relaxed expectations of EU-level associations, justify a weighting factor of '3'.

FACTORS 4 AND 5: MEMBER/NON-MEMBER ACTIVITY IN BRUSSELS; COUNTER-LOBBYING BY MEMBERS

Associations that exist alongside their own members, or a derivative constituency (i.e. firms, in the case of associations of associations), in the environs of Brussels find their role in political representation diluted and risk being bypassed. This phenomenon exists in sectors populated by large firms where either the large firms themselves are present in Brussels, or/and the associations to which they belong at national level use the resources they make available to fund a presence. Small firms, or national associations representing a constituency of almost exclusively small firms, do not have a presence in Brussels on the grounds of resources.

Annual entries in the *European Public Affairs Directory* provide one source of information about 'member' activities in Brussels. It should be regarded as a useful indication, rather than a definitive source on 'member' activities. The listings depend upon the information sources available to the *Directory*, and the willingness of the listing constituency to accept an entry and to keep it updated. Some members may have a presence in Brussels, but the concept of a 'public affairs presence' is riddled with definitional difficulties. Some use office facilities of a divisional or local base in the Brussels environs, whereas others use a public affairs consultancy. Those using the latter service choose from a tariff of services which may or may not include direct representation to the EU institutions. While most of the companies and national associations listed are members of EU business associations, a very small proportion (e.g. Virgin) are not.

Geographical issues also need to be taken into account in estimating 'member presence'. Interests from nearby bases in Paris, Bonn, Amsterdam and the Hague are within easy travelling distance of Brussels, and may therefore be frequent visitors without requiring a permanent Brussels presence. A further issue concerns the role of the Belgian associational members of EU federations, who, strictly speaking, all exist alongside their EU associations. Some of these may be used informally by the network of members within an association, perhaps on an issue basis, to talk directly with EU political institutions. On the whole, however, the author's own interviews conducted with Belgian national associations do not reveal any kind of 'bypass' role. Instead, they suggest a role as a loyal member driven by a small-country mentality which emphasises the need for an EU-wide organisation in the presence of larger forces. Some do provide resources to assist EU associations, and the implications of this are considered in the debate on 'autonomy' later in this chapter.

With these extensive caveats in mind, some caution should be exercised in interpreting the information available from the *Directory*. Nonetheless, some useful rough and ready observations can be made. The 2001 edition of the *Directory* (Landmarks, 2001) lists 245 firms with corporate public affairs offices in Belgium, and 51 national business associations from European countries[2] based in the area. Of the remainder of the firms with a listing but based outside Brussels, 50 of the 86 firms (58%) are UK-based, while 20 of the 51 Brussels-based national business associations (39%) are from Germany. These statistics yield two interesting observations. The strength of the UK corporate sector in Brussels reflects the British tradition of pluralist 'lobbying', while the strength of German associations reflects the dominant tradition and status of associations as agents of 'interest intermediation' in German 'public affairs'. This tradition suggests that the UK firms are more likely to act as unreserved free agents in EU public affairs. Whilst German national associations with a Brussels presence do, from time to time, engage directly with EU institutions, they play a more reserved role in bypassing their EU associations. This is because of the very strong tradition of German collective action through associations, and the status of the agents as associations with certain loyalties to associative traditions. These latter factors reinforce the point made in Chapter 1 about the ways in which German interests can dominate EU associations, but also a wider point about the ways in which interests are 'socialised' by the system in which they are embedded. At its simplest, if bypassing the association is normal behaviour in the UK, so it will be reproduced in Brussels, whereas German traditions also inform the behaviour of German players in Brussels. At a more theoretical level, these points would be taken by 'new institutionalist' scholars of European integration as evidence of 'sociological institutionalism', in that the belief systems of the actors derive from the social environment surrounding them.

Those who engage in the bypass often justify their activities by reference to the weakness of their EU association and its inability to come to common positions. Yet much of the source of the 'associational bypass' lies with the fragmented architecture of the EU institutional system, with multiple points of access and dispersion of power facilitating access by outside interests. This lack of 'stateness' of the EU disables the ability for the EU to provide the necessary

---

[2] This figure excludes localised business associations, such as the Food from Brittany association, national chamber of commerce offices, the professions and other non-business organisations, and the two Belgian business associations listed.

patronage required for associational strength (Chapter 1). There is no sector in which relations between the EU and business is conducted wholly through an associational intermediary. Nonetheless, there is some variation in the associational patronage of EU institutions, with different parts of the EU institutions possessing different capacities to structure associations, or displaying different policy behaviour towards associations. For instance, the European Commission may hand out places on key advisory committees only to members of EU associations, making membership essential. Historically, this has been most evident in agriculture and food, which has a disproportionate share of such advisory committees and where the historic preference of the Commission to engage with associations has been strongest. Where the Commission possesses policy competencies, under certain types of circumstances it may seek to encourage industry to use its EU association as a vehicle of self-regulation, in preference to the use of formal rules (see factor 7 below). This degree of patronage can be a source of associational strength and provide a significant membership incentive.

Another source of the 'associational bypass' is the low level of resourcing available to EU associations in comparison with some of their members, which is largely a function of the restricted tasks invested in EU associations for political representation (Chapter 1). Some of these members seek to maintain the EU association on a low level of activity out of a preference to manage their EU public affairs directly with the EU institution, and view their principal task of membership to prevent the association from doing any harm. This scenario is not untypical where there is a high degree of significance attached to competing technical standards, discussed later in this chapter. In these circumstances, a lobby 'free for all' between members is often the outcome. In some cases, associations seek to manage this diversity through the use of qualified majority voting, or minority positions, although these cannot be used where the consequences for members are so high that the likely response to a loss of a vote would be a significant exodus from the association. Some associations also seek to bring their large firm members with a Brussels presence under their umbrella by holding a regular series of coordination meetings with the public affairs personnel concerned. These meetings may reduce the frequency of bypass, and even make it possible that the resources of members could sometimes be used to enhance the efforts of the association. However, it does not remove the reality that firms who have invested in a public affairs presence will expect to see their outlay justified, and those who occupy these positions on behalf of firms are likely to find agendas to do this. Even the most intense example of coordination – the 'Monday morning meetings' hosted by EFPIA, the European Federation of Pharmaceutical Industry Associations, for its large-firm members in Brussels – do not seem to have altered the reality of bypass, or lessened the problem in comparison to other sectors with similar contexts. Public affairs managers of large firms will find their own networks, and in some cases these exist outside of the scope of the association. In the automobile sector, where every single member company of ACEA, the European Automobile Manufacturers Association, has its own public-affairs capacity in Brussels, the personnel involved have established their own monthly meeting club of 'Brussels Automobile Representatives', with sufficient identity for each member to refer to it by its acronym, BAR. These company offices have been inspired, as much as anything, by the presence of competitors and the need to keep an eye on each other. Part of this task concerns using ACEA to ensure that no one company uses the association to gain a competitive edge over its rivals by getting its technical product standards adopted as the basis for industry-wide regulation.

In any scenario, a high degree of member activity in Brussels is likely to lead to the loss of autonomy by the EU association, because its activities are more closely monitored, and the member has an enhanced ability to exercise influence over the activities of the association.

Factors 4 and 5: Member activity in Brussels, and counter-lobbying by members, will considerably affect the cohesiveness of an association. As the discussion above indicates, each of these factors are linked, though qualitatively different. Member activity in Brussels may be coordinated to some degree with the association, though the result is generally a loss of strength to the association. On the other hand, counter-lobbying is a stage further, which is much more of a direct threat to the authority of an association. Consequently, this latter activity was given a higher weighting, '4', than was member activity, which was weighted '3'. Nonetheless, because these factors are to some degree present in most sectors because of the fragmented architecture of the EU, neither attract the highest rating in a study examining the factors responsible for variation in the capacity of EU business associations.

FACTOR 6: INVOLVEMENT WITH CROSS-SECTORAL ORGANISATIONS

The cross-sectoral organisations offer the opportunity for an EU association to get its key interests taken up under the badge of another, business-wide, organisation with a higher profile. The chemical and pharmaceutical industry associations, CEFIC and EFPIA respectively, are proficient users in this way of working parties within UNICE, the Union of Industrial and Employers' Confederations of Europe, and in doing so are able to get many of their own positions carried forward in the name of UNICE. In order to work this route, an association needs to be sufficiently endowed with monitoring capacity to spot the opportunity, and to arrange the personnel to contribute to the working party. Once a position is articulated in the name of a wider organisation, so it helps contribute to the climate of consensus for an idea within the association from which it originates.

> *Factor 6*: A close involvement with cross-sectoral organisations is both a cause and symptom of associational cohesion. The opportunities it presents justifies a weighting factor of '3'.

FACTOR 7: SPECIFIC REGULATORY REGIME ACTIVITY AND/OR SEEKING REGULATION; SELF-REGULATION

One of the reasons for existence for most associations is either the stimulus of, or the search for, regulation. From the former perspective, Staber and Aldrich (1983) note from their observations of American life that most associations formed since the 1950s have done so in order to oppose 'burdensome overregulation'. Another American author, Cathie Jo Martin, chides associations for behaving 'like feisty two year olds, very good at saying "no" to regulations that offend their narrow self-interests' (Martin, 1997: 399). From the opposite perspective, Crouch draws attention to the ways in which associations owe their very existence to their roles as a working part of an entire system of regulation (Crouch, 1998), and whose activities are geared towards seeking, and the maintenance of, regulation. In this account, state regulation is used by associations to shield business from competition, or by firms to seek competitive advantage over one another in the design of regulatory systems. In essence, these authors are describing contrasting systems of economic management, based either on liberal markets where lobby pluralism prevails (e.g. the Anglo American model), or regulated order, where associations are an embedded feature (e.g. Germanic Europe). In the former, associations are one 'channel' of 'interest representation', whereas in the latter they are the principle interlocutor between the state and business in an embedded system of 'interest intermediation'. State regulation provides a role for associations, whereas markets emphasise firms as political actors (Zysman, in Coleman and Grant, 1984).

Whilst there is much to commend these two ideal types as analytical devices, in practice the maintenance of market competition requires an extensive system of government regulation. That is, 'deregulation' in search of a market system leads to 'reregulation'. The EU system is of interest because it has followed this path, where a system of nationally protected markets has been replaced by a system of open liberal markets. In order to achieve this, a framework of competition policy rules has been passed to outlaw the former and achieve the latter. This process of de- and reregulation is central to this analysis because of its impact upon associations. For instance, Lehmkuhl (2000) describes how the process of EU deregulation removed the *raison d'être* of a German transport association, because the purpose of that association was to maintain a protected competition market. In Olsonian terms, the association was a 'rent-seeker' which had extracted authority from the state to run a cartel, distorting the efficient allocation of wealth by interfering with free-market competition. EU associations have to live in an entirely different system in which free-market ideas are sacrosanct. Crouch notes how adjustment to deregulation leads to a change from corporatist-type systems to pluralist pressure politics, particularly where interests diverge on the impact of deregulation. Certainly, deregulation can intensify competition between members in markets, and make it more difficult for them to work together collectively (Gosman and Forman, 2001). Large firms are usually in favour of deregulation to achieve open markets because they have the resources and infrastructure to operate across borders, whereas medium-sized firms which have operated in protected national markets stand to lose most from intensified cross-national competition. The respective efficiencies that these perspectives involved were the very foundation for the single market, and the reason for the formation of the European Round Table of Industrialists (ERT). ERT sought to build and extend deregulated liberal markets inside the EU in the interests of large (principally, manufacturing) firms, although it too went through a protectionist phase when it came to competition from outside the EU (Chapter 5). Taking arrangements in one sector as a further example, the EU Electricity producers association EUR-ELECTRIC was initially formed to oppose European Commission attempts to deregulate the European electricity market, while IFIEC (International Federation of Industrial Energy Consumers) sprung a European regional branch dedicated to seeking EU Electricity deregulation. These contrasting interests in liberalisation and protectionism can be found within many EU associations, sometimes resulting in a stalemate whereby the association is reduced to a 'damage-control' role while the members undertake their competing lobbying activities (described in factors 3 and 4 above).

Whilst Gosman and Forman (*op. cit.*) are generally pessimistic about the impact of deregulation upon collective action, they also note the ways in which it can provide opportunities to take on functions previously undertaken by the state through self-regulation. Taking the opposite view, Crouch (1998) contends that deregulation is destructive to self-regulation. It is worth debating these contrasting perspectives because there are substantial pockets of associational self-regulation at the EU level, and substantial ambivalence towards the concept among the EU institutions. Most recently, there is a significant challenge to it from the European Commission in the current debate on 'alternative regulatory models' in the run up to the 2001 White Paper on Governance (WPG). This debate takes the form of examining ways of enhancing the legitimacy of EU regulation, and, whilst it raises the prospect of parcelling out further regulatory capacities, it seeks to broaden participation beyond business interests to other interests in civil society. It also raises questions about the accountability of self-regulation in the guise of proposing an alternative model of 'co-regulation', in which the EU would share regulatory authority with outside interests in a power-sharing model, and regulate the involvement of outside interests. The debate has split business interests. Some sense a loss of power, while others do not interpret it as a significant threat. Among the latter category, the response of one Brussels-based manager of a national business association was typical in reflecting to me that 'we can live with co-regulation, but we like self-regulation even more'.

A useful starting point in the analysis of self-regulation is the observation that it can vary substantially in its content and significance. Where self-regulation is 'licensed' through powers granted by the state for monopoly regulation, such as national associations of some professional groups (e.g. doctors, lawyers), associations can become extremely powerful. No association at the EU level is in such a position, because of the lack of 'stateness' of the EU to grant such monopoly powers, and the fragmentation of EU powers. Similarly, there are very few EU associations that bind members to these agreements and exercise the disciplinary powers over them to police these agreements.[3] Where self-regulation operates at the EU level, it does so alongside that at the member-state level. Nonetheless, there are a variety of models of development, ranging from those that substitute for formal legislation by the agreement (and perhaps prompting) of the EU institutions, to those that are little more than codes of good practice developed by business in the hope that they might forestall regulation. The examples provided below go through this spectrum, from strongly to weakly developed, with analysis in each case of the impact upon collective action in the domain concerned.

The European Advertising Standards Alliance (EASA) was founded in 1992 in response to a direct challenge from the then Competition Commissioner, Sir Leon Brittan, to demonstrate that advertising in the Single Market could be successfully dealt with through self-regulation. It has met this challenge, to the extent that Leon Brittan, prompted by sources in the industry reflected in a public speech in 1998 that 'the work of the EASA has reduced the need for legislative intervention' (Gray, 2001). More recently, Commissioner Byrne put on record in one of his own addresses that 'this is a fine example of how effective self-regulation can be' (*ibid.*). EASA could seek no finer a recruitment and

---

[3] Perhaps the nearest to it is the scheme operated by the European Tyre and Rim Technical Organisation (ETRTO), on behalf of tyre manufacturers, discussed later in this chapter.

membership retention sergeant, or encouragement for interests to work through their association rather than to bypass it. The second example is that of EFPIA, the European Federation of Pharmaceutical Industry Associations mentioned earlier, whose code on the self-regulation of standards of selling to medical practitioners establishes some of the basic principles on which national codes should operate. In doing so, the code acts as an agent of harmonisation, and an agent of development in the few cases where codes are absent, and, like advertising, its presence has also acted as an alternative to EU legislation. Nonetheless, the code has done little to strengthen the EU association further, because most of its members already subscribe to a code operated by the International Federation of Pharmaceutical Manufacturers' Associations (IFPMA). EFPIA's strength somewhat predated self-regulation, and the function has not significantly added to its capacities or prevented a recent trend whereby its large-firm members have increasingly bypassed it in establishing their own dialogue with the EU institutions. This is consistent with Bennett's interesting contention that self-regulation is of interest more to associations than it is to companies, for whom the core task of representation is of greater interest (Bennett, 2000).

Both the advertising and pharmaceutical industries display an established history of self-regulation at the national level, and it has not been difficult for either industry to reproduce tried and tested strategies. Something similar exists in the chemical industries, where there are a number of examples of responsible care standards at the EU level which have developed from those at the national level. In the main, these standards have been developed at the initiative of the industry itself, both in response to criticisms raised by environmental public interest groups and for market utility in response to green consumerism, whereas those in advertising and pharmaceuticals developed following challenges laid down by the European Commission. Consequently, these standards, while useful and potentially preemptive, have added little to the capacities of the association. A final example of self-regulation concerns a scheme operated for euro payments by EuroCommerce, which illustrates an observation by Grant that the existence of self-regulation doesn't mean that the association will be significantly less fragmented, and that fragmented industries are also capable of delivering self-regulation (in McCann, 1995). However, there is little evidence to support Crouch's point that deregulation is destructive of self-regulation. Rather than leading to the dismantling of national self-regulation, EU-level self-regulation tends to have built on, or supported, that which exists at the national level. On the whole, the evidence supports the more opportunistic view taken of deregulation for self-regulation by Gosman and Forman.

Factor 7: From the discussion above, the reasons for assigning a '5' weighting to regulation and its related concepts will be apparent.

FACTOR 8: ASSOCIATION USED FOR LOBBYING

Chapter 1 introduced the idea that membership of EU business associations can be driven both by habit, and by reason. Of the latter category, the discussion above indicates a diverse range of reasons for using EU business associations. At the minimalist end of the spectrum, membership is informed by the need to be in a position to exercise influence over the positions of the association. At the maximalist end of the spectrum can be found a reliance upon the association to conduct political representation with the EU institutions. Whilst there is substantial diversity to be found within and between associations, and a host of causes, some analytic order can be imposed. In sectors and domains where members have little alternative, such as those in which large transnational firms are absent, the association will provide the mainstay of lobbying activity. The lack of an alternative does not on its own, however, imply cohesion, although in SME-dominated sectors the association does have an enhanced capacity to control its agenda (Chapter 1). In sectors where members have sufficient resources to have their own public affairs management capacities, the association exists alongside other active channels employed by their members. A number of other sectoral characteristics (such as homogeneity), and characteristics of the association itself (such as the degree of autonomy, predicting variations in reliance upon it for lobbying, are identified below, while others (such as varieties of regulation) have been reviewed above.

Factor 8:   This factor was one of the easier ones to assess during interview questions, with respondents asked to quantify their estimated degree of reliance upon the association for lobbying. A higher degree of reliance by members upon the association for lobbying will tend to be related to associational strength and cohesion. Because the absence of an alternative does not in itself imply cohesion, the weighting factor is no more than '3'.

FACTORS 9, 10, 11 AND 12: ASSOCIATION USED BY MEMBERS FOR INFORMATION; TRANSACTION-COST SAVINGS; TRUST BETWEEN MEMBERS; DEGREE OF EU IDENTITY IN GLOBAL TRADE

All associations collect and generate information for, between and from their members, whether about political activities and non-activities by EU institutions, those with a different category of interests, or the members themselves. To some accounts, the costliness of information collection is a principle cause of associations, in that the cost of gathering it is often beyond the capacity of any one member. Information costs are a core component of transaction-cost economics

(TCE) introduced in Chapter 1, and associations can play a central role by lowering information costs. These costs include those involved in measuring the value of a product, including the costs involved to produce it. Solutions include collective action to address the problems arising from these costs, including collective production of information, regulating the uncertainties in the political environment (in attempts to seek political advantage from it), and fostering trust between members as an alternative to more costly contractual mechanisms in conducting business relationships. Hollingsworth, Schmitter and Streeck record that:

> In all modern economies, companies have associated with each other to collect information about production levels and prices, to conduct joint research and development, to promote standardization, to engage in technology transfer and vocational training, to channel communication and influence to state agencies, to formulate codes of conduct, to negotiate with labor, and even to decide on prices, production goals, and investment strategies. (1994: 7)

EU associations undertake some of these activities, but by no means all because their ability to do so is restricted by European competition policy, and by the restricted ambition of their members in seeking organisations which are primarily concerned with political representation. In addition, the status of many EU business associations as associations of associations means that only some of these tasks will be of interest to their members, whereas those associations which organise firms might find that their members have a greater breadth of interest in the above list. Even then, many large firms can satisfy these sorts of activities themselves, without having to rely upon associations (Sabatier, 1992). Whilst transaction-cost economics has been held to explain much about the world of business associations, it therefore has limitations which are both specific to the EU level, and general. In a major review of its application, Schneiberg and Hollingsworth (1991) conclude that it contributes little to our understanding of how associations emerge or die, but has much to offer in the analysis of the 'middle stage', that is how associations develop. The first, emergence, stage is dominated by the stimuli of states, and/or political entrepreneurs, rather than the needs identified in the stage above, though these needs explain how the association develops from start-up. The use of TCE in the analysis of EU associations should be undertaken with all the above qualifications borne in mind.

Associations have featured in a number of European competition policy cases. Those that have reached the Courts have included cases involving national associations in wood pulp (Court of Justice, 1993)[4] and the European Broadcasting Union (Court of First Instance, 1996).[5] In three separate cases in

---

[4] Joined Cases C-89/85, C-104/85, C-114/85, C-116 & 117/85, C-125-129/85.
[5] Joined Cases T-528/93, T-542/93, T-543-93, T-546/93.

the mid–late 1990s, hefty fines were handed out to industry operators in the print, steel and cement sectors, with the two EU associations concerned in the steel and cement sectors, EUROFER and CEMBUREAU, implicated in the findings of cartel-like behaviour. In a number of other cases known to the author, the Competition Directorate of the European Commission has intervened to demand changes in the statutes of the association to prevent anti-competitive behaviour. One of these cases involved an association which supplied a good essential for trading, but which allowed entry by invite only, and which charged double first-year membership fees to deter new market entrants. The statutes were duly changed. A further example of the way in which the assertive use of competition powers has significantly restricted the ability of EU associations is provided by an association organising multinational firms in a highly concentrated sector, in which a competition-policy lawyer is hired to sit in on each and every meeting of the policy-making executive. This anxiety not to cross the boundary into 'anti-trust' arenas may be partly fuelled by the activities of US companies in Brussels. From the list supplied in the Hollingsworth *et al.* quote above, prices, production levels and goals, and investment strategies, are definitely excluded from the scope of EU associations.

Notwithstanding this key point, there are a number of things that EU associations can do to lower transaction costs. A very small number, such as the European Association of Aerospace Industries (AECMA), broker and coordinate joint research and development activities for their members. A more mainstream activity is self-regulation, discussed above, although it is unlikely that these arrangements exist at the EU level to the same extent as those at the national level.[6] Conducting negotiations with labour is another, whether under formalised 'social partnership' arrangements, or voluntary 'social dialogue'. For the non-specialist reader, a summary of these processes is worthwhile because they have contributed to the capacities and membership appeal of a number of EU business associations. UNICE is a formal 'social partner' with CEEP (Centre for Enterprises with Public Participation – read 'public sector employers') and ETUC, the European Trade Union Confederation, in which the organisations are empowered under the EU Treaties to negotiate agreements in labour-market fields which can later become EU legislation. Other business associations play a supporting role, including UEAPME (European Association of Craft, Small & Medium-Sized Enterprises) which joins UNICE at the negotiating table and in reaching positions on behalf of business, and, where necessary, those which have a more specialised constituency such as EuroCommerce, or the tourism association HOTREC (Confederation of the National Hotel and Restaurant

---

[6] Litvak (1982) found that 60 per cent of a sample of 101 business associations in Canada, for instance, had established some type of self-regulatory capacity.

Associations in the European Communists). Business has become involved in the making of binding social legislation as a pragmatic way of expressing its self-interest (the key mechanism is the Commission's position of 'negotiate or we'll legislate') to brake the development of EU-level social policy, or engage in damage limitation. But for the representative associations involved, the added incentive has been organisational development in that membership of them is essential as a means of influencing the positions they adopt. A number of business organisations have a semi-licensed, designated role through their identification in Commission policy documents[7] which assess the competencies and capacities of each of the organisations involved in cross-sectoral social partnership, designating a status as a 'first-level' or 'second-level' social partner. For UNICE, its role as a social partner now forms one of its two core aims. At the sectoral level, where there is no route to binding legislation, some associations have sought a role in social dialogue as a way to enhance their appeal to members and potential members, even if the reality is little more than participation in discussion about relatively uncontentious issues.

Some coordinate participation in standardisation through the framework of the European standards bodies, CEN (Comité Européen de la Normalisation), CEN-ELEC (European Committee for Electrotechnical Standardisation), and ETSI (European Telecommunication Standards Institute), in which experts from the relevant industries drawn from the national level join with others to undertake the technical harmonisation required for product standards to be consistent with single-market rules. However, whilst the coordinating role of EU associations varies considerably, the role is not greater than that of coordinator, and in consequence this does not add much to associational capacities or appeal *vis-à-vis* their members. In some instances, however, sectors have created their own EU technical organisations, either to develop intra-industry standards, or to contribute at a high level of technical expertise to EU debate. The European Tyre and Rim Technical Organisation (ETRTO) is in the first of these categories. It met the need among European tyre producers to seek enhanced access to global markets by 'exporting' European tyre standards on a worldwide stage, and as a measure to protect these standards from dilution by demands from automobile manufacturers placed upon any one member to develop customised products. No changes to these standards are permitted until they have the agreement of the industry-wide body. In consequence of the factors, the organisation has a membership density of 100 per cent. CONCAWE, the Oil Companies European

[7] COM (93) 600, *Communication Concerning the Application of the Agreement on Social Policy*; COM (97) 241, *Communication from the Commission on Promoting the Role of Voluntary Organisations and Foundations in Europe*.

Organisation for Environmental and Health Protection, is a slightly different type of organisation designed to satisfy the technical requirements of legislation affecting the oil industry, and to meet the challenge of the Green lobby through engaging in debate by scientific intervention. Whilst technically independent of EUROPIA, CONCAWE's offices and libraries are physically linked to it.

The role of CONCAWE is indicative of the central role in information provision played by EU associations, to take the final area of activity described by the quotation taken from Hollingsworth, Schmitter and Streeck. It is one of a number of EU associations that generate high-quality information, and for many associations this is their most significant contribution to EU public policies. AEA (the Association of European Airlines), CEMBUREAU, EURELECTRIC and EUROFER are examples of associations that have substantial technical information departments which have made the European Commission, and in part their members, dependent upon them. In some cases the information they produce is unique, akin to the niche specialisms which associations search for and occupy described earlier in this chapter. AEA, for instance, generates substantial information for its members on issues affecting the airline industry, such as remuneration of pilots and average charges per turnaround. EURELECTRIC produces statistics about changes in net generating capacity, consumption and production on a per country basis, and volumes of trading, facilitating strategy formulation by members. Provided the information produced is of sufficient depth, as well as uniqueness, then the association concerned will be able to develop resource dependencies from users and substantial independent capacities. These qualities yield the necessary autonomy from which associations derive strength.

In order to achieve this autonomy, Coleman makes the point that the information processing required of the association to order and coordinate should be neither too complex or too little (Coleman, 1988). In processing information from their members, the members are placing a high degree of trust in the association to protect potentially sensitive commercial information from other members. As is evident from the discussion below, trust is also a key factor in lowering transaction costs for members, and in developing associational autonomy. These capacities can only exist if the associational staff in the technical information department are independent of any one member, and a resource truly belonging to the association. If, on the other hand, such staff are seconded from one of the members, particularly where an association represents companies, other members are unlikely to have sufficient trust to hand over commercially sensitive information, which in turn will prevent the association from developing its unique information services.

Trust in others decreases the uncertainty of transacting. This concept has its roots in classical democratic theory, where associations help their participants understand and empathise with others, and the interdependencies created result in consideration and mutual adjustment. As Newton summarises the concept:

> they [i.e. associations] teach empathy, the art of compromise and co-operation ... they encourage the habits ... of civilised social relations. They breed and enforce reciprocity – it is difficult to behave badly in business if you know you will meet your victim at the golf club dance on Saturday. (Newton, 2001: 206)

Business associations can help firms come to terms with one another (Lall, in Doner and Schneider, 2001a). Trust fostered through business associations can in turn reduce the costliness of acquiring information, which forms a substantial portion of the costs of transacting. In particular, they can help firms reduce the time spent acquiring information, address information asymmetry (when one party has more information that the other), and reduce the need to use formal contracts to regulate business relationships between others. Part of the attraction of participating in associations concerns the quality of the network, and if this network can foster trust between members, so that trust can reduce the need for formal contracts in exchanges between firms. There is a ring of plausibility to this, though it should not be overestimated. Firstly, firms do not rely upon trust, and use contracts as a failsafe mechanism. Secondly, national associations do not contract between one another, and the value is restricted to those associations that organise firms. Thirdly, levels of trust, and the use of it to govern social relations, varies significantly between western European countries, from the Nordic countries where it is high, to the south of Europe where it is lower (Newton, 2001). Thirdly, EU associations differ in the type of company personnel they bring together. Some network public affairs managers, whereas others bring together technical experts as well through their working parties, and others still may even bring together chief executive officers. Not all bring together the parties in firms who are involved in forming business alliances with other firms. However, for those engaged in public affairs management, participating in networks is seen as essential, and can be a source of both social opportunities and of identity, which over time can generate 'club' loyalties. Apart from these 'soft' benefits, the activity of networking is of sufficient importance that the prospect of the loss of access to it helps to keep members in the association, even though the time taken to participate in associations may sometimes appear to exceed the benefits it seems to yield. The prospect of losing access to a potentially vital nugget of information in the future may explain why public affairs managers live through the tedium of participation. The importance of the cost of non-membership to associational cohesion is developed below.

A final factor in this section concerns the role of the association in providing its members with political intelligence, the value they place upon it, and its role in membership. Most members have a grumble of some kind about the way in which their association passes information to them about EU-related activities. Most frequently the complaint is that they get too much information, too little of it is really focused or useful – more aimed at protecting from a later charge of 'you should have told me about this' – and it is sometimes too late. Most large firms with their own public affairs management capacity do not rely upon their EU association as their mainstay, but use their resources to do so themselves or to contract the job out to a public affairs consultancy. Similarly, many national associations have more resources than the EU association to which they are affiliated, and use a mixture of their affiliation and their own channels of information. Some have a dedicated EU affairs department, while others distribute EU responsibilities as a horizontal function amongst staff with other categorised specialisms. On the whole, members with small resources of their own are more likely to be reliant upon the EU association. However, the increasing availability of information through the internet, often customised by suppliers for business users, has reduced the reliance by most members upon their EU association as an information source. In any event, the EU has always been noted for its openness and accessibility. Where the EU association has developed a sufficient capacity to generate unique information at a level of depth, so dependencies will be generated among members, irrespective of size.

Factors 9, 10, 11 and 12:   A higher degree of reliance by members upon the association for information will tend to be related to associational strength and cohesion. Because most members obtain their information through a number of channels, and because of the ease of obtaining this, information (factor 9) attracts a weighting of '2'. Transaction costs (factor 10), on the other hand, is weighted as '3'. While this factor is superficially attractive, its lack of applicability for the context of many EU associations restricts its weighting. The degree of trust between members (factor 11) receives a higher weighting of '4' because of its obvious applicability for cohesion, although the degree of subjectivity involved in identifying its presence means that it cannot reliably attract a higher weighting. The final factor, the degree of EU identity in global trade, is provided by the example of ETRTO. Whilst this example provided a highly valuable insight into how associational cohesion can be provided by an EU identity in global trade (factor 12), the rarity of EU specific identity in the teeth of global ownership patterns of major industries makes it difficult to assign a weighting in excess of '1'.

FACTOR 13: OTHER INCENTIVES, FOR EXAMPLE ACCESS TO OTHER ORGANISATIONS

An earlier debate in this chapter identified how the European Commission can support EU associations by providing them with a 'gatekeeper' role for EU advisory committees. There are an estimated 2000 of these, of which 1000 are officially registered and 300 of these are defined in law through their establishment by the Council. They provide access for an estimated 50 000 participants (van Schendelen, 1998). Whilst advisory committees vary in their importance, access to them can still be prized. Some exert important influences, and can be demanding of their members. Others are less so, and provide the opportunity for members to undertake activities which can enhance their status back home, undertake travel to another country, and to have a day out of the office in a setting less demanding than their usual routines, funded by generous expense allowances. In the most extreme cases where EU associations bring together members so divided that building collective opinion would be pointless, access to EU advisory committees can provide the most important reason for associational membership. The EU association EUROPECHE (Association of National Organisations of Fishing Enterprises in the EU) is the closest example of this type known to the author.

As the earlier discussion on the limited, coordinating role of EU associations' standards bodies revealed, this factor should not be overestimated in informing membership, and acting as an agent of cohesion, of such associations.

> *Factor 13*:   Access to other organisations can be the greatest 'glue' factor for associations, but in the absence of others is insufficient on its own to be an independent source of cohesiveness. Consequently, the factor attracts a weighting of '2'.

FACTORS 14 AND 15: AUTONOMY FROM MEMBERS; THREAT OF EXIT

> Effective associations need to be resourceful and autonomous to define and sustain a course of action over the long run that is neither linked exclusively to the immediate preferences of their members nor dependent on the policies or partners and agencies external to their domain. (Schmitter, 1992: 438–9)

A senior Commission official in DG Enterprise recounts how one EU business association manager came to a meeting and said he couldn't talk with them as he had been mandated not to co-operate (White, 1997). An association needs to have autonomy from its members to be able to bring value to them, and act as a useful partner to political institutions in EU policy-making. Those that are too closely controlled by their members become a mouthpiece for their short-term demands, making them too rigid to be long-term governance partners. Those that have acquired some autonomy from their members' short-term demands have the flexibility to participate in policy-making with EU institutions, and in acquiring this property are able to bring value to their members. A key measure of autonomy is the ability of an association to resist the short-term demands of its members, while constructing a sense among them as to what their long-term interests are. That is, the association is constructing the preferences of its members, rather than being a prisoner of them. It may withstand short-term member pressures in order to undertake their long-term interests. This is what Coleman had in mind with his idea of a 'policy capable association':

> as a participant in policy-making, it is more that the sum of the interests of one or the other. It takes on a life of its own and is able to rise above the short-term, particularistic interests of its members. It not only can see beyond, to the medium and longer term, it can define for its members what their interests are within this broader perspective. (Coleman, 1988: 51)

To be able to undertake this delicate task, an EU association needs to avoid capture by any one specialised interest, to exceed its members appreciation of EU public affairs, to have an independent supply of resources of funding and expertise, a decision-making structure which provides insulation from control by any one member, and highly skilled leadership. The preceding discussion in this chapter and from Chapter 1, summarised here, suggests how, in general, EU associations struggle to have all of these qualities. Going further than this, McCann (1995) suggests that EU associations have little autonomy, and are 'mere conduits of communication'. The high degree of specialism common to them means that they are too closely tied to the interests of their members, whereas associations with a more encompassing reach across different types of interests are more insulated from the demands of any one specialised constituency. Low membership numbers arising from specialism can be a source of low autonomy. This is one advantage that cross-sectoral organisations such as UNICE have over narrow, highly specialised associations representing the interests of, say, vegetable protein, or natural sausage casing manufacturers. UNICE also has a relatively large number of members – currently 33 – in comparison to most sectoral associations of national associations. Given that most EU associations are still associations of national associations, the autonomy of the population is generally low because, by design, most have a small number of members, that is based around the associations from 15 member states. Whilst there is some variation to this, in that some admit from beyond the member states and some have different categories of members, the point remains that most EU associations have a relatively small number of members in comparison to their national counterparts, and that this in turn reduced associational autonomy.

Sharing the public affairs space in Brussels alongside their large-firm members, and among members with multiple points of access to decision-making, severely restricts the ability of EU associations to be able to monopolise the tasks they undertake. Taken as a whole they have a relatively low level of resourcing in comparison to national associations because of their restricted roles as political representatives. This low level of resourcing increases the levels of dependence that they have upon their members. Because their functions are narrowed to those of political representatives, they are dependent upon membership subscriptions for their incomes, and do not tend to have an independent supply of 'own resources' from the sale of other services that might commonly be found among national trade associations. Many EU associations are also young in comparison to their national counterparts and have not built up substantial reserves or property interests in their own premises; rather, as relative latecomers to Brussels, many are victims of high property rents rather than owners of property which acquired later value through booms. Worse still, some are dependent upon facilities provided by their members.

A consequence of this low level of resourcing includes the commonplace practice to use secondments from members. In turn, this may undermine the key quality of trust that other members are prepared to invest in their association, such as handing over potentially sensitive information. In order to build up such trust, members need an extensive history of involvement in the associations (Doner and Schneider, 2001b). Associations require an independent and secure supply of financial resources and the ability to develop their own independent source of expertise, including staff, in order to increase the dependence upon them by others. Once this independence is acquired, associations can draw upon the information from their members to supplement their own resources rather than to rely upon them (Coleman, 1988).

Associations also require space to think, develop and take risks, and those that exist alongside large firm members in Brussels are inevitably too closely monitored by them. This presence also carries a high risk that the EU association will be too closely controlled by a small number of members. To avoid this, associations need to insulate themselves by design, such as spreading affiliation fees and voting influence between members. This is a very delicate balance to achieve. Over time, a number of associations have sought to address their lack of resources by admitting large-firm members directly. This can help in spreading influence where they exist alongside national association members, but where the association becomes a representative only of company members, so it is possible that a small number of large members will come to dominate. The obvious balance to this is a constitutional spread in the weighting of votes. Although very few associations vote much, the constitutional presence of voting rules concentrates the minds of members, and governs their tactics in coming to collective decision-making. However, if the votes are spread too thinly, the large-firm members, who expect to have more influence over the work of the association than their smaller brethren, may pose a threat of exit. In order to avoid this there is either a constitutional link between firm size, affiliation fees and votes carried, or an informal trade-off between large-firm and small-firm members whereby the former agree to bankroll the association in return for more influence. The challenge is to provide this weighting of influence towards those who provide the lion's share of resources without making the association too dependent upon any one category of member. Another constitutional possibility is to ensure that seats on the key decision-making structures are elected by the membership as a whole, rather than acting as delegates from individual members, while another is to ensure that decisions do not require the approval of all affiliates (Schmitter and Streeck, 1981).

Like those from other contexts, EU associations have wrestled with these concepts. The extent to which these design features work are also mediated by the extent to which there are established relationships between members. Whilst there are very unclear implications to be drawn from the management literature of the relationship between participation and effectiveness, it is possible that group-centred decision-making and a strong sense of collegiality may form part of the recipe for success. On the one hand, the diverse geographical constituencies of EU business associations, and their confederate structures providing for low membership numbers and a sense of collegiality, give them an advantage over their national association counterparts in diluting the concentrating of influence. On the other hand, the low levels of resourcing they endure have provided incentives for them to trade the spread of influence in return for more resources, with the consequent loss of autonomy.

Browne's work on the specialisation of associations leads to a more controversial conclusion about the impact of resourcing upon associational cohesiveness. A high degree of specialism, and co-operation, is seen in his work as a function of a low degree of resourcing. On the basis of this tendency to specialise, Browne suggests that 'interest groups with scarce resources develop great cohesiveness of purpose, function, and operation' (Browne, 1977: 56). Another way in which associations cope with low resources, he reasons, is to limit the demands of the membership. This is done by simple mechanisms such as providing information leaflets to fend off individual enquiries, and more complex mechanisms such as 'farming' the membership to gain supporters on policy matters. This latter concept refers to the ways in which the secretariat of an association leads its membership in the views they take of their interests. In this, the demands of the membership are reduced and conflict is avoided. This is a controversial perspective on how associational autonomy is developed which is contrary to much conventional wisdom (i.e. the perspective that high autonomy results from a stable, significant and secure independent resource base), but it does at least provide an interesting link between resourcing and the leadership provided by an association.

The resource of leadership is the most difficult to tie down. The role of association general secretary is a highly exposed position, in that he or she is always walking a tightrope between trying to provide leadership to the construction of member preferences, whilst at the same time being seen to reflect by their actions their articulated wishes. Resisting short-term demands in favour of someone's interpretation of longer-term interests is extremely difficult in democratic organisations, and one which requires a great deal of trust in personnel and the vigorous support and protection of the President to act as a patron. This is a very narrow tightrope from which a fair few fall, in that the world of EU associations has a relatively high number of 'blameless victims', of chief executive officers (CEOs) who are highly regarded for their competence and vision but who fall victim to internal membership politics. This scenario is more frequent where power is concentrated in an association. In the eyes of a powerful large-firm member whose demands are being resisted by an association chief officer, 'leadership' has become a 'principal–agent problem' whereby the principal (paying membership) has lost control over their agent (CEO) and an opportune moment to reassert control. Where an association is viewed in these terms, so it is a symptom that it is unlikely to have obtained the requisite autonomy (Coleman, 1988). Only where there is a high degree of trust in the personnel, and between members, is the exceptional 'space' likely to be granted to the associational leadership to pursue the agenda they have defined as being in the long-term interests of members. This elusive quality of trust is one that is built up over many years from repeat interactions; there are no short-term recipes. Once again, the trust–autonomy nexus seems to have a key role to play in the effectiveness of associations.

Where EU associations are able to develop autonomy, it stops short of the extent to which it can be developed in national associations. Continuing the quote above, Coleman argues that:

> Within this degree of autonomy, the association may even assume responsibility for directing and in some cases controlling and sanctioning the behaviour of its members. (Coleman, *op. cit.*)

National associations have frequently developed these capacities in return for 'licenses' to undertake the lion's share of regulation through self-regulatory schemes. These sanctions range from 'naming and shaming', through to fines or even expulsion. Pestoff (2000) describes a scheme of 'direct debit fines' with Swedish associations, in which members are required on joining to provide their full banking details together with authority for the association to levy fines direct from the account without further recourse to the member.

The inability of EU institutions to 'licence' their associations deprives them of a key source of autonomy. Associations that have the visible approval of state authority have the ability to keep their distance from their members. By the other token, associations also need to keep a distance from their 'state' interlocutors in order to preserve their autonomy, a problem in highly corporatist systems such as Austria. Few EU associations ever get close enough to the EU institutions to run this risk.

The depth of the concept of autonomy can be gauged from its link to 'institutionalist' theories of integration, in that these concepts focus on the ways in which the perceptions of those who participate under their umbrella are constructed by these institutions. In this usage, the associations are the institutions that 'socialise' the preferences of their members, constructing a sense of what these interests actually are, and in the course of this alter members' behaviour. If associations can do this, they are in a uniquely powerful position.

Factors 14 and 15: The degree of autonomy from members is a '5' weighting factor. The potentially devastating threat of exit justifies a similar weighting of '5'.

FACTOR 16: EUROPEAN OR NATIONAL MARKETS

A prerequisite for EU associations to be effective concerns the degree to which their members are involved in cross-border trading. If a membership constituency is encamped in national markets they are unlikely to be well-organised at the EU level, whereas if the principal markets of members are cross-border, they are likely to look to their EU association before they turn to national associations. Those encamped in national markets seek protectionism, whereas those with cross-border trading issues support liberal trade that is the single-market ideal. The first grouping regards the EU as part of the problem and turns to their national government for help and transitional protection, while the second sees it as the solution and seeks to use the full authority of the EU. This relationship between perception of the EU as a threat or opportunity, and resourcing of EU associations, can also be witnessed in groups representing the professions. Ideology and common identity can be considerable factors of 'glue' for associations.

Despite enterprises encamped in national markets being at a natural disadvantage in associational representation at the EU level, they at least have the cohesion of common identity and interests. A more common scenario is where an association has a mixed constituency of interest, and in these circumstances there is unlikely to be cohesion. While most associations contain a mixture of both, most also lean one way or another. Those with a genuine balance are likely to struggle.

Factor 16:   The profile of trade is a factor significantly associated with associational effectiveness. Sectors with a profile of trade in European, rather than national, markets are more likely to invest in their EU association. Of all profiles, associations with a genuinely mixed constituency of interests in cross border, or national, trade, have the classic conditions for conflict. The obvious potency of this factor justifies a weighting of '5'.

FACTOR 17: COLLECTIVE CLOAK

At a superficial level, all members of EU associations confirm the presence of this factor – that is, the conveyance of interests to the EU institutions under the weight of a collective badge and identity – as a reason for membership, and many cite it as the principle reason. But given that political representation is the purpose of EU associations, it cannot be a factor of variation. Where it is, the concept of a 'collective cloak' is a little different to the sense in which members perceive it. A useful interpretation is where there are issues of sufficient controversy in the domains in which members operate for them to avoid association with issues directly. Typically, these issues arise in arenas of open public debate, and involve the association engaging public opinion. Environmental and labour-market domains are two of these, where companies, in particular, may find it too exposing to take a tough public position, and associations provide them with the opportunity to do this. On their own they are too exposed to articulate what they really want, but under the guise of an association they may be able to articulate these views. This may help explain the sometimes pejorative public perception of associations; one company public affairs manager based in Brussels told the author that 'you cherry pick your issues, taking up those you want to be associated with, and leave your association to pick up the crap.'

Another interpretation of the collective cloak is where a company requires the appearance of a collective identity. This happens in sectors that are so highly concentrated that there may be just a handful of firms, or even just a single firm. Cawson (1992) cast the European Association of Consumer Electronic Manufacturers (EACEM) he then knew as an organisation dominated by Philips and Thomson, although EACEM has since undertaken considerable changes to its membership constituency. A more up-to-date example concerns the way in which some of the highly specialist food associations are dominated by Unilever, described in Chapter 1.

Factor 17: As a generalised concept, the 'collective cloak' is of little value in explaining variation in EU business associations because in this sense it is the principle purpose of their existence. But in its more specialised usage, the concept can explain some variation in cohesiveness, although the very specific senses in which these arise justify a weighting of no more than '1'.

FACTOR 18: COMMON ENEMY

The stimulus of an 'opposition' ranks alongside factors such as 'regulation' and 'state patronage' in explaining the reasons why interests organise collectively. These factors are linked, in that business associations are typically involved with regulatory issues, and regulatory issues typically produce (or threaten to produce) winners and losers, and thus competitive politics (Lowi, 1964). Much associational membership depends upon external threats, in that it is much easier to rally a known constituency against the threat of the loss of an existing good, than it is to mobilise a latent set of beneficiaries. When costs are narrowly concentrated but benefits widely distributed, an entrepreneur usually arises to champion a cause, and an organisation emerges to fight the case. When both losses and benefits are narrowly concentrated, the classic result is competitive interest-group politics (Wilson, 1995). Where political systems produce fragmentation among the organisation of business interests, such as the EU, so there are incentives for competition among the rest.

Most commonly, business organises collectively because labour organises into a union. At the European level, just as important stimuli to business interest organisation are the presence of competing interests in the product chain, and public interests which contest the corresponding one of business. As well as providing stimuli to the start up of business interest associations, these factors also sustain cohesion. Groups tend to respond better to external political problems than with internal economic ones; there is nothing like a 'common enemy' to keep members together. The European Chlorine Association, EUROCHLOR, for instance, organises members who produce chlorine by using mercury, and the intensive use of this has been a persistent target of attack by direct-action environmental groups such as Greenpeace. Whilst there is an alternative production process, a large constituency of members need to buy substantial time to convert to it, and the 'glue' of the association is therefore a sharply common focus to undertake political action to achieve this aim. The reason for collective action in this case is, very tangibly, the 'bottom line' to doing business and is all too apparent to members. In other cases, members will need the guidance of the association to locate the threat and interpret it for them. Wilson reasons that:

> If threats arise from outside a group, they tend to increase group cohesiveness and integration and heighten the attraction that group members feel towards one another. This effect will be greatest when members perceive the threat in similar ways. (*op. cit.*: 309)

This latter point places some emphasis upon the issue debated in the discussion on autonomy above, that is the ability of associations to be able to shape preferences of members as to what their interests actually are. Associations have the task of locating the information, defining it as a problem, providing interpretation and 'selling' the threat to members. Where a threat is perceived in similar ways, so it will enhance the cohesiveness of the EU association.

Factor 18:   The presence of a 'common enemy' attracts a weighting of '5'.

FACTORS 19, 20, 21, 22, 23 AND 24: EXTENT OF COMPETITION WITHIN SECTOR; OVERCAPACITY; DEGREE OF CONCENTRATION; DISRUPTIVE M&A ACTIVITY; DEGREE OF FIRMS OF SIMILAR SIZE; TECHNOLOGY DIVISIONS

These concepts are about the impact of market-driven influences upon associability. The extent of competition in a sector is related to its degree of maturity, which in turn affects the extent of merger and acquisitions (M&A) activities, and the degree of concentration. The impact of these linked factors upon associational cohesion are well-mined in the subject literature, although they require adaptation to the world of EU associations. For some, associations were founded so as to regulate competition, and rank alongside 'governmental regulation' and a 'common enemy' in importance to explaining why associations emerge (Schneiberg and Hollingsworth, 1991). The mainstream literature on competition is well-summarised by Doner and Schneider, who, citing Adam Smith's famous remark about reaching for your wallet whenever two businessmen get together, note that capitalists have always attempted to prevent 'ruinous competition' in product and factor markets (Doner and Schneider, 2001a). In this, they draw links to the emphasis placed by transaction-cost economics upon the ways in which associations can reduce the costs of transacting. These include the ways in which the state is used by associations to shield business from competition, and to the historic role of associations as agents of cartels. Indeed, there is near unanimity in the general literature that the structure of competition, and changes to it, whether in product or labour markets, gives rise to attempts to manage it through associations (see, for instance, the review of sources such as Chandler, Schmitter and Brand, Grant and Coleman, van Waarden, and Hanley, in Schneiberg and Hollingsworth, 1991). Consequently, competition in markets is seen as a factor of variation among the functions, capacities and performance of business associations (Traxler and Schmitter, 1994).

Despite this emphasis, there is little analysis upon the ways in which competition makes it more difficult for business interests to work together. Market turbulence and sudden and unanticipated changes in demand lead to pressures on competition, and pressures on associations to reform themselves (Schneiberg and Hollingsworth, 1991). Associations can, and do, change where once protected market sectors are opened up to competition (Lehmkuhl, 2000; Doner and Schnieder, 2001). In the EU context, in particular, there needs to be a greater focus upon the ways in which changes to competition brought about by the European single market impact upon associability. The entire single-market project was specifically designed to unleash the forces of competition as a strategy of wealth-creation. On the one hand, change in the structure of competition may encourage resort to comfort and guidance mechanisms like collective action. On the other, the logic of intensified competition does not always facilitate intensive action, and some working EU-related examples of these difficulties are provided below.

The most obvious among these forces has been the tendency to make large firms larger. There is certainly an established literature describing the role of large firms as individualistic actors in EU public affairs (Coen, 1997; Cowles, 1995), and some pockets of speculation about the impact of intensified competition upon firm behaviour such as Traxler's early analysis (1991) about enhanced individual action in industrial relations. Undoubtedly, there are aspects of the increase in unit size of large firms that might facilitate collective action. On balance, however, the review conducted earlier in this chapter has been upon the ways in which large firms with sufficient resources to dedicate to EU public affairs management are disruptive to the capacities of EU associations. In addition, whilst the process of mergers and acquisitions is underway, so associations are losing members, resources and established relationships with participating individuals. Similarly, as was argued earlier in this chapter and in Chapter 1, EU competition policy has significantly narrowed the scope of EU associations. Although there are models drawn from the member-state level[8] whereby associations can continue with their historic roles in setting the pattern for

---

[8] Bruyn provides the example of the UK Association of the British Pharmaceutical Industry, and its involvement in that country's Pharmaceutical Price Regulation Scheme.

governing the market in which free competition arises (Bruyn, 1991), such capacities to organise markets never developed in the first instance in EU associations. The structure of EU competition and its grounding in mutual recognition may also unleash competition between national standards (Schmitter, 1997), which can also make EU associability and consensus-building in EU associations difficult. Competition can be managed without the use of associations, and there are European structures such as product standardisation which can help business do this. In all these respects, the EU environment of competition is disruptive to associability.

Areas of business activity with a high degree of competition clearly throw up some barriers to competition, although the impact of competition is tempered by the presence or absence of other factors that create the perception of a common interest. Competition tends to be fiercest at early stages of the product cycle where rival firms struggle to bring research downstream, to establish markets, and to get key technologies adopted as common product standards. Typically, this process is disruptive to collective action. In very early stages of the product market, where entrepreneurial start-ups have played a significant role in seeking applications for the research, collective action is extremely difficult. Later, there is a process of concentration where those SMEs that have delivered promising technologies are acquired by larger firms, or enter into strategic alliances with them. At this stage of the product cycle it may be typical for firms to cluster around rival technologies where the intensity of competing interests is so great that the collective association is unable to take sides. In this situation, the task of firms is to keep the association from being hijacked by the competing interest, and an informal settlement emerges to keep the association neutral, and quiet. The competing interests then cluster around rival *ad hoc* coalitions. Pijnenburg describes such a scenario in the early 1990s, where the information technology sector split into two rival camps around an EC directive on the legal protection of software[9] (Pijnenburg, 1998). These camps became established into issue alliance networks to the extent that they acquired characteristics such as names. The alliance each firm joined depended upon the process from which its technology derived, which in turn dictated its interests as in favour, or against, the directive. SAGE (Software Action Group for Europe), a coalition of companies such as IBM, Philips, Siemens, Apple, Microsoft and Lotus, supported the directive which required the agreement of the copyright holder before products could be developed based on a process of 'reverse engineering'. ECIS (European Committee for Interoperable Systems), containing firms such as Bull, Uni-sys, Amstrad, Olivetti, ICL and NCR, opposed the directive because their products depended upon the use of ideas, concepts and logic that lay at the basis of computer software.

---

[9] Directive 91/250/EEC of May 1991.

In the automobile sector, similar divisions between the interests of firms in lean-burn engine technology and catalytic converters led to paralysis of EU representative associations and became a significant change agent for collective action (McLaughlin and Maloney, 1999).

The organisation of interests concerned with gene-splicing technologies has also displayed many of the historical characteristics of progression along the product cycle. Small, national associations primarily organised start-up firms. Eventually these formed an umbrella EU association, the European Secretariat of National Biotechnology Associations (ESNBA). Large firms with separate interests, and more skilled in public affairs management, organised directly at the EU level into a different association, the Senior Advisory Group Biotechnology (SAGB), initially hosted by the established chemicals industry association, CEFIC. As the sector matured, so did the landscape of business interests and eventually the two associations came together as one, EUROPABIO (European Association for Bioindustries), with a dual membership category of large firms and national associations.

There may be circumstances where the development of new technologies is so sensitive that it is difficult for firms to participate collectively, because to ask an association to take up a particular position may reveal to competitors key information about the strategies and product development of a rival. In one association where this issue is live, however, the members continue with their affiliations, so the General Secretary believes, to spy on competitors and to gain broader market intelligence. Thus, members continue with their affiliation for information, but do not use the association to take up political positions on their behalf. Competition arising from new technology development thus restricts the role of the association, with membership less for the positive benefits of membership than to avoid the costs of non-membership, discussed below. The particular association concerned is well-established, but the development of a new technology in the sector has completely changed its usage by members. Whilst these circumstances are relatively severe, fierce competition between members may well be a general factor limiting the scope of associational life. Nonetheless, it should also be noted how firms at each other's throats in the marketplace and in the courts can and do work alongside one another effectively in EU business associations. Butt Philip and Porter give the example of Unilever and Mars, confronting each other in the courtroom over the storage and display of ice cream in freezer cabinets in retail outlets, or locked in media 'soap wars', yet who are also close partners in associations such as AIM, EUROPEN (European Organisation for Packaging and the Environment) and ERRA (European Recovery and Recycling Association) (Butt Philip and Porter, 1997).

As with competition, there are divided perspectives on the impact of concentration upon associability. On the one hand, some degree of concentration is desirable to avoid the problems associated with fragmentation and low resource yields, yet at the other extreme concentration can undermine the reason for associability, or associations become front organisations tied to a particular firm. Drawing on experiences from the national level, Boléat (1999) suggests that an ideal company constituency for an association to manage is between 100–400. This ideal constituency would be composed of firms of a similar size where there is closer alignment of interests (for a review see Bennett, 1999, citing the work of Blank, Hirschman, Olson and Salisbury) than between those of sharply diverging size such as the 'corner shop to supermarket' constituency organised by EuroCommerce. Membership mechanisms such as peer pressure and coercion can work in membership profiles of this sort (Olson, 1965; Wilson, 1995; Bennett, 2000). Indeed, it is this factor which prompts Mizruchi (1992) to link high concentration with associational cohesion. Similarly, Bowman finds that levels of industry concentration is a factor explaining variation in associational cohesiveness, in that low profit margins and overcapacity stimulate co-operation (in Bennett, 1999). In these circumstances, firms look to associations to manage the overcapacity problem, and it is for this reason that well-endowed associations exist throughout the steel and cement sectors, including those at the European level. This factor is developed and qualified by Schneiberg and Hollingsworth who observe that it is chronic or sudden overcapacity, in conjunction with high fixed costs, that create powerful incentives for price cutting, and firms turn to associations in an attempt to control prices (e.g. cartels), production and investment (Schneiberg and Hollingsworth, 1991). The airline industry is an example of a sector in which there can be sudden overcapacity in conjunction with high fixed costs, and where well-endowed associations can usually be found.

Factors 19–24:   Where there is overcapacity (factor 20), so associations have a strong role to manage the problem. Overcapacity and sector maturity results in concentration (factor 21). Whilst extreme concentration can have negative effects upon collective action, a high degree of concentration is conducive to it. Both factors therefore attract a weighting of '5'. On the road to concentration there is a process of mergers and acquisitions (factor 22), and these can lead to a loss of resources for associations. Whilst extreme fragmentation may provide associations with some degree of autonomy, anything between this and high concentration may make it difficult to organise their constituency, locate common interests and attract sufficient resources. A key appears to be firms of similar size (factor 23), with a weighting of '4', just outside the 'top bracket' of independent variables. The impact of mergers and acquisitions upon associability, and technology divisions, may be temporary, justifying a weighting of '2'. More controversially, the degree of competition (factor 19) also attracts a weighting of '2', lower than might have been weighted by other analyses because its impact at the EU level can weaken associability.

FACTOR 25: PRONENESS TO LOWEST COMMON DENOMINATOR POLICY POSITIONS

As collective entities, all business associations seek to find common positions between their members, and in doing so the outputs almost always reflect some degree of compromise. The particular proneness of EU business (and agricultural) associations to lowest-common-denominator positions was noted in the very first analyses of them (Sidjanski, 1967; Caporaso, 1974; Kirchner, 1981; Butt Philip, 1985; Grant, 1990). Variation in this factor provides the cause for this book, and the principle causes for it are reviewed in this chapter. In the research interviews each of the respondents was asked to assess the extent to which the association in question was subject to this factor, and to identify some of the possible causes. It provides the basis for many of the qualitative insights provided by the quotes in Chapter 4. As a symptom, it may itself be the cause of other contributory factors; Coleman notes a 'chicken and egg' question, whereby states may be reluctant to provide lowest-common-denominator associations with patronage or public status. This issue is apparent from a presentation by a senior Commission official, David White, who reflected that:

> when we are looking at technical and legislative problems we are more interested in getting a rich position than in getting a unique position. I think we understand that a European trade association is representing a very wide range of different interests and they do not invariably speak with one voice and have a single view. Some opinions that we have received have worked on the lowest common denominator principle, so that by the time they reach us they are of precious little use; they do not say anything. It would be much better to say 'well some of our members think this and some think that', because this builds up the picture and helps us to understand what is going on. (Bennett, 1997b: 10)

In this account, the principal role of EU associations is to highlight the differences between members, acting as an early warning indicator of potential differences when issues reach decision making in the Council of Ministers. Later, in Chapter 5, a more subtle version of this concept is described in considering the way it is used in UEAPME as a tool to deflect unwanted policy initiatives.

Some types of EU associations, and particularly those whose legitimacy is based on representing a breadth of constituency, are particularly oriented towards consensus-seeking (Chapters 1 and 5). However, Wilson suggests that all associations lean towards consensus for reasons of organisational survival:

> goal definition tends to be divisive – the more specific the objective, the greater the likelihood there will be disagreement over it within the organisation ... maintenance needs are better served by having vague or broadly stated goals ... highly general purposes ... when very few persons are available to do the work of the association, they must walk a tightrope between organisational maintenance and goal achievement, but by walking they usually lean to one side, so that, if they fall, they fall on the side of keeping the association alive. (Wilson, 1995: 217)

Similarly, Wilson argues that consensus-driven organisations are an inevitable result of the ageing process:

> The history of most associations shows that legal-rational rule tends to replace patrimonial rule. The principles of legitimacy necessary for the support of patrimonialism are usually short lived or unstable ... associations then become bureaucratised, routinised, and open to the accusation of being ponderous, undemocratic, or conservative. Age produces conservatism in organisations. (*Ibid.*: 223).

These perspectives provide a somewhat pessimistic scenario for the role of business associations *per se*. Writers drawn from a perspective of business science have contributed a more relaxed and sometimes more optimistic scenario. Authors from this perspective have contributed most to a much neglected aspect of interest-group research, through organisationally-based analysis of internal operation and administration (Browne, 1977, 1990; Litvak, 1982). Litvak (1982) sees the tendency towards organisational maintenance as a natural function of the need for long-term stability and predictability in relations with political leaders, government bureaucrats, other association executives and contesting organisations such as labour unions. In this account, business interest associations in all settings are oriented towards organisational maintenance.

There has been something of a tendency to produce broad-brush generalisations of EU associations, often pejorative in nature. This tendency can be found among business interests, the EU institutions, and in some of the older literature. Sometimes this has been based on no more than a case study of a single sector (see, for instance, McLaughlin's 1993 study of the automobile sector). Yet the literature reveals considerable variation (see, for instance, the extensive case study collections in Pedler and van Schendelen, 1994; Greenwood, 1995; Pedler, 2001; the literature review conducted by Greenwood, 1997; and the cases and reviews in Eichener and Voellzkow, 1994). Similarly, results presented in Chapter 4 of this book indicate considerable variation in performance between associations in different business domains, ranging from those characterised above, to some EU associations which are the mainstay of business/EU relations at the desire of both EU institutions and their members. The task is to map the variation, while the intellectual task is to explain it.

There was at one time also a tendency to see the proneness of EU business associations to lowest-common-denominator positions as largely restricted to being a problem of the 'association of associations' structure. Certainly, associations whose credence is based around a high membership density are more prone to this than are exclusive 'clubs' of members (Chapter 1), because their authority stems from their ability to speak on behalf of a wide constituency of members. These organisations are more likely to be federated in structure, although it is wide of the mark to see the lowest-common-denominator proneness as the exclusive domain of federative structures. This sort of analysis dates from a period where there was a growth in large-firm activity in Brussels, and coupled with it was an over optimistic expectation that the problem would be resolved by the emergence of direct-membership organisations to represent them. The 'federations bad, direct representation good' movement, reviewed in Chapter 1, found an outlet in the formation of the European Round Table of Industrialists (ERT) in 1983[10] (Chapter 5).

Among other perceived advantages, direct representation seemed to offer the prospect of speedier decision-making than federated structures were capable of, and, because these organisations were likely to attract firms of a similar size (large), might aid cohesiveness. These concepts, together with the general activation of large firms in EU public affairs in the 1980s and beyond, led to the reform of the largest EU association, CEFIC (European Chemical Industry Council), in 1991, to admit large firms. In turn this provided one catalyst for change throughout the domain of EU business associations, involving the admission of large firms alongside national association members, or the development of organisations dedicated to the representation of large firms (Chapter 1). These brought their own problems of sectoral division and lack of encompassingness, and from the mid-1990s onwards the trend was back to inclusiveness, with a move towards dual-membership structures. In 1996, CEFIC extended this trend through a set of reforms that produced a tripartite structure in which EU associations in the

---

[10] Membership of ERT is for chief executive officers rather than corporate affiliation, though ERT publicity makes more of the names of the companies they represent, and in either case the principle is direct representation of company interests.

chemical 'family' were included as well as national associations and firms. Today, the federated organisational structure remains the most common (Chapter 1). Whilst this trend back to inclusiveness primarily reflected the limitations of direct-membership organisations reviewed above, it also reflected the realisation that direct-membership structures were not a panacea to the lowest-common-denominator problem. This was often because of the presence of the same structural issues of division derived from sectoral or market forces reviewed earlier in this chapter which had afflicted federated structures. Direct membership structures were an attempt to find a solution to the wider problems of lowest common denominators, rather than a solution to the causes. As reviewed throughout this chapter, these causes lie beyond the reasons that led to the direct-membership movement.

Factor 25:   The proneness of EU business associations to lowest-common-denominator positions was a question explored by the interviews reported in Chapter 4. The factor was weighted '4' because it is an issue that affects all business associations to some degree.

FACTORS 26, 27 AND 28: MEMBERSHIP FOR BENEFITS OF MEMBERSHIP; EXTENT OF EVALUATION UNDERTAKEN; MEMBERSHIP TO AVOID COSTS OF NON-MEMBERSHIP

The author has long noted a discrepancy between the perspectives of the secretariat of EU associations on the one hand, and their members on the other, as to the value that is sought from membership. EU associations frequently state that their members are hard-headed, cost–benefit evaluators of their membership, constantly seeking value for money and added value from their subscription. Interviews with their members do not confirm these perspectives. As reported in Chapter 4, few undertake any evaluation of their membership, and few could imagine any scenario that would result in them leaving the association. As argued in Chapter 1, EU associations exist for the very specific purpose of helping their already politically active members manage EU public affairs, and these members do not require an extensive range of special membership incentives and services. Most EU associations include national associations for whom collective action is normal political behaviour – 'the thing to do'. So, also, is political action for large firms, who almost always take the opportunity to participate in EU associations when the opportunity presents itself, and often provide the leadership for these associations to function (Chapter 1). The impression of frequent member evaluation held by some EU associations might be explained by the pressures and sometimes threats which their members articulate in trying to get their way. As a methodological reflection, it might also convey the right impression in an interview of a responsive organisation attuned to business principles and language.

Collective political representation and all the activities and benefits associated with it provide distinct and positive incentives for membership. Membership of an organisation that does all these things, and provides a high quality network, requires little explanation. Even where members are unable to identify these benefits, the costs of non-membership such as the loss of ability to influence the positions of the association, the potential loss of a nugget of vital information or incurring the displeasure of others, means that membership arises and prevails. All of these factors are in their own way Olsonian-type membership incentives.

Factors 26–28: The presence and strength of membership incentives, whether for positive benefit or the cost of non-membership, impacts upon the cohesiveness of associations. Following the logic of the cost of non-membership, the absence of member evaluation is positively associated with cohesion, whereas its presence implies a threat of exit. All of these factors are weighted '4', important in their own right but slightly below the top rated factors such as degree of regulation, overcapacity, and a 'common enemy'.

The weighting of factors, and the association with governability of each factor, is presented in summary form in Table 3.1. The use to which the second column, the association with governability, is put is discussed further in Chapter 4. It is presented here because it reflects a summary of the discussion above.

Table 3.1 Factor weightings and factor association with governability

Weighting	Association with governability (+ or −)
5	
Degree of specialism in the product chain	+
Specific regulatory regime activity/ seeking; self-regulation	+
'Common enemy'	+
Threat of exit	−
Overcapacity	+
Degree of concentration	+
Autonomy from members	+
European or national markets	+ (European)

Table 3.1   Continued

Weighting	Association with governability (+ or −)
4	
Counter-lobbying by members	−
Prone to lowest-common-denominator positions	−
Membership to avoid costs of non-membership	+
Membership for benefits of membership	+
Extent of evaluation undertaken	−
Degree of firms of similar size	+
Trust between members	+
3	
Issue-niche organisation	+
Involvement with cross-sectoral organisations	+
Association used for lobbying	+
Membership density	+
Transaction-cost saving	+
Member/non-member activity in Brussels	−
2	
Association used by members for information	+
Extent of competition within sector	−
Disruptive merger & acquisition activity	−
Other incentives, e.g. access to other organisations	+
Technology divisions	−
1	
Collective cloak	+
EU identity in global trade	+

4 Results and Analysis: Domain-Based Associations

This chapter presents the results from interviews with EU associations, their members and non-members. Focusing the discussion in this chapter on domain-based associations, it identifies the patterns that arose in assessing causal factors of variation and similarity between associations in their ability to unify their members' interests, and to secure the compliance of their members with associational goals, that is their 'governability'. Given that most of these factors are present in the external environment of associations and are matters over which associations have little influence, the results presented in this chapter should not be read as an appraisal of these organisations. Thus, the results presented in Tables 4.1–4.3 in the pages that follow, obtained from following the methodology outlined in Chapter 2, are not 'league tables' of 'associational effectiveness' or 'performance', rather they seek to assess the factors of governability proposed in Chapter 3, to help identify the causal factors of variation between associations. Because of this, the discussion of results in this chapter after presentation of the tables occurs without a detailed focus upon any one individual association.

'Simple' assessments examine the extent to which a particular factor is present in an association (Table 4.1), whereas 'weighted' assessments make reasoned assumptions about the importance of factors (Table 4.2), multiplying each score obtained from Table 4.1 against a weighting for the particular factor, justified in Chapter 3 (Table 3.1). The interviews allowed most associations to be assessed against each factor. Where this was not possible, the assessment was left blank and the factor was not included in calculating the average 'score'. Thus:

- In Table 4.1, the final row, the *average governability score*, equals the sum of all scores for an association divided by the number of factors for which a score was recorded.
- In Table 4.2, the score for the *weighted average governability*, equals the score for each association recorded against each factor in Table 4.1 multiplied by the weighting for each factor, divided by the number of factors for which a score was recorded.

The 'score' against each value reflects the value attributed to it from the discussion in Chapter 3, summarised in Table 3.1. Thus, where a factor was associated positively with governability, a high degree of presence of that factor attracted a high value on the scale 1–5; for instance, a very high degree of specialism attracted a score of '5'. Where a factor was associated negatively with governability, a high degree of presence of that factor attracted a low value on a scale 1–5. Thus:

- A high degree of a negatively-rated factor attracted a low value on the scale 1–5. For instance, a high degree of counter-lobbying by members attracted a score of 1 or 2.
- A low degree of presence of a negatively-associated factor attracted a high value on the scale 1–5. For instance, an association judged to be subject to a low threat of exit, attracted a score of 4 or 5.

Using this method enabled a high score to be associated with a high degree of governability, and vice versa. These scores from Table 4.1 and 4.2 are summarised in Table 4.3. The data presented in these tables represent a high volume of information, and are therefore worthy of considerable scrutiny. However, it should also be recalled that the numeric values assigned in Table 4.1 were subjective values, based primarily upon interview assessments. They are therefore an aid to assessment of the factors, and to locating common factors. They indicate 'ordinal' degrees of differences, rather than a literal presentation of 'interval' data in their own right. They are not intended to be an instrument of precision 'measurements', but rather a guide, or aid, to analysis. Nonetheless, it is intended to extract the maximum utility from them. Normally, the median might be the appropriate descriptive statistic to use in association with ordinal data, such as a 1–5 scale. However, use of the median in Table 4.1 would produce an almost universal value of '3' throughout, which would not do justice to the variations in governability revealed through the allocation of scores. Consequently, the arithmetic mean was used to provide such an indication.

The first column in Table 4.3 indicates a mean score of 3.4 (see also Table 4.4, later in this chapter). Thus, the mean governability score for this group of associations is slightly above the middle point of 3, justifying a conclusion that this sample of EU business associations have medium levels of governability. This finding is of some significance in its own right; that is, provided that this sample has some degree of representativity of the sample as a whole, EU business associations have neither low nor high degrees of governability. The upper quartile of associations showed an average of 4.2, while the lower quartile showed an average of 2.6 (Table 4.4).

The first column in Table 4.3 provides the best method of assessing the weightings attributed to particular factors, in that this represents unweighted placings. Nonetheless, Table 4.3 indicates a broad similarity in the placing of associations from the results obtained by application of the 'simple' (Table 4.1)

Table 4.1 Variations in governability of EU business associations: simple assessments

	ACE	ACEA	AEA	AIM	AMCHAM-EU	CAOBISCO	CBMC	CEA	CEFIC
Degree of specialism in the product chain	5	5	4	5		4	4	4	3
Issue-niche organisation	5	5	4	5		4	4	4	3
Member/non-member activity, in Brussels	3	1	2	2	2	3	3	3	2
Counter-lobbying by members	5	1	1	3	4	3	2	2	2
Involvement with cross-sectoral organisations	5			5			4		5
Specific regulatory regime activity/seeking	5	3	4	4		5	5	3	5
Association used for lobbying	5	1	2	4	3	4	4	2	5
Association used for information	5	2	3	2	4	4	3	2	5
Prone to lowest common denominators	5	1	2	3		3	3	2	5
Membership to avoid costs of non-membership	5	1	4	5	4	4	4	4	5
Membership for benefits of membership	5	1	2	5	4	4	4	2	5
Common enemy	5	2	2	5	4	4	4	1	5
Collective cloak	5	2	2	4	5	4	2	1	5
Extent of evaluation undertaken	5	4	4	3	3	5	3	2	5
Threat of exit	5	4	4	2	3	5	3	3	5
EU identity in global trade	4	3	2			4	4	2	5
Degree of firms of similar size	4	5	4	4	4	2	3		5
Membership density						3	4		
Overcapacity	3	4	4	2				3	4
Extent of competition within sector	4	3	4	2		2	3	4	4
Degree of concentration	5	3	4	3		3	4	4	4
Disruptive merger & acquisitions activity	4	2	1				2	3	2
Technology divisions		2							3
Autonomy from members		1	1	4	3	3	2	3	4
Trust between members		1	1	5	4	2	3	3	4
European or national markets	5	5	5	5	5	3		5	5
Transaction-cost saving									4
Other incentives, e.g. access to other organisations									4
Average governability score	5	2.6	2.9	4	4	4	3.3	3	4

Table 4.1 Continued

	CEMBUREAU	CEPS	CIAA	CIMSCEE	COCERAL	COLIPA	COPA/COGECA	CPIV	EAAA
Degree of specialism in the product chain	5	5	1	5	5	2	2	5	5
Issue-niche organisation	5	5	2	5	5	3	2	5	5
Member/non-member activity, in Brussels	4	2	2	2	4	3	1	4	3
Counter-lobbying by members	4	2	2	3	4	2	1	2	3
Involvement with cross-sectoral organisations	5		4						
Specific regulatory regime activity/seeking	4	4	5	3	5	5	5	1	5
Association used for lobbying	5	2	4	2	4	4	3	3	4
Association used for information	5	3	4	3	4	5	3	3	4
Prone to lowest common denominators	4	3	1	4	4	3	1	2	4
Membership to avoid costs of non-membership	2	3	5	5	4	3	4	2	4
Membership for benefits of membership	5	2	3	4	4	5	1	3	4
Common enemy	5	4	4	1	5	5	4	4	4
Collective cloak	5	4	4	5	4	5	4	2	4
Extent of evaluation undertaken	5	4	4	5	5	3	4	2	5
Threat of exit	5	4	5	5	5	4	4	1	5
EU identity in global trade	4		5						
Degree of firms of similar size		4	2	5	4	2	2	2	4
Membership density	5	4	3	5			4	2	
Overcapacity	5				4	3	4		2
Extent of competition within sector	5	4	2	4	4	2	3	2	2
Degree of concentration	5	4	3	4	3	2	3	2	4
Disruptive merger & acquisitions activity	4	2	3	3		2			2
Technology divisions			3						
Autonomy from members	4	2	1	3	3	2	2	2	5
Trust between members	5	2	2	4	3	2	1	1	4
European or national markets	3	4	4	4	4	4	3	2	5
Transaction-cost saving					5				
Other incentives, e.g. access to other organisations							4		
Average governability score	4	3	3	4	4	3	3	3	4

	EACEM	EAT	EBankU	EBroad-castingU	ECA	ECF	ECSA	EDA	EEO
Degree of specialism in the product chain	3	2	3	4	5	4	4	3	5
Issue-niche organisation	3	5	4	5	5	4	4	3	5
Member/non-member activity, in Brussels	2	1	1	3	4	4	3	3	3
Counter-lobbying by members	2	2	1	4	4	3	2	3	3
Involvement with cross-sectoral organisations									
Specific regulatory regime activity/seeking	4	4	3	4	4	3	2	5	5
Association used for lobbying	4	1	3	4	5	4	4	3	5
Association used for information	3	1	2	4	4	4	4	3	4
Prone to lowest common denominators	2	1	1	4	3	3	4	2	3
Membership to avoid costs of non-membership	4	3	5	5	3	4	3	3	3
Membership for benefits of membership	3	1	2	5	3	4	4	3	5
Common enemy	3	2		3	4	2	4	3	5
Collective cloak	3	3		4		3	4	3	4
Extent of evaluation undertaken	2	2	1	5	3	4	4	5	4
Threat of exit	2	1	5	5	2	2	4	4	2
EU identity in global trade	4		3		5	4	5	4	
Degree of firms of similar size	4	4	4	5	2	3	5	3	3
Membership density	3	2	4	5	2	3	5		2
Overcapacity	2				4		5		2
Extent of competition within sector	3	3	2	4	4	3	4	4	1
Degree of concentration	4	4	2	5	2	4	4	4	3
Disruptive merger & acquisitions activity	2		2	5	3	4			
Technology divisions	2	5	2		3	4	4		3
Autonomy from members	2	1	1	4	4	3	4	3	4
Trust between members	2	3	2	4	2	3	4	3	3
European or national markets	4	5			3	5	5	3	4
Transaction-cost saving					4				
Other incentives, e.g. access to other organisations									
Average governability score	3	3	3	4	3	4	4	3	4

Table 4.1 Continued

	EFA	EFCA	EFPIA	EGTA	EMOTA	ERT	ETRTO	EURATEX	EURELECTRIC
Degree of specialism in the product chain	4	5	4	4	3		5	2	2
Issue-niche organisation	4	5	4	4	4	5	5	2	2
Member/non-member activity, in Brussels	5	4	2	3	3	4	4	4	2
Counter-lobbying by members	4	3	2	3	3		4	3	2
Involvement with cross-sectoral organisations						4			
Specific regulatory regime activity/seeking	4	4	5	5	5		4	4	5
Association used for lobbying	2	3	4	3	4		2	4	3
Association used for information	1	3	3	5	4		4	4	4
Prone to lowest common denominators	2	3	3	3	4	4	5	2	3
Membership to avoid costs of non-membership	2	4	5	5	5		4	4	5
Membership for benefits of membership	1	3	4	5	4	5	5	3	3
Common enemy	2	3	4	4	4		2	4	2
Collective cloak	2	1	4	3			1	3	3
Extent of evaluation undertaken	2	3	5	2	4	2	5	3	4
Threat of exit	2	1	5	2	4	3	5	3	5
EU identity in global trade		4				4	5	5	1
Degree of firms of similar size	3	4	4	4	4	5	5	4	4
Membership density	2	2	5	2			5	3	4
Overcapacity								4	4
Extent of competition within sector	2	2	3	2	4		5	2	3
Degree of concentration	2	2	4	4	4		5	2	5
Disruptive merger & acquisitions activity			2	3			3		2
Technology divisions							4		
Autonomy from members	3		3	3	3	2	3	2	2
Trust between members	2		4	1	4	4	4	3	2
European or national markets	1		5	3	2	5	5	3	3
Transaction-cost saving			4	4	5		5	3	
Other incentives, e.g. access to other organisations					4				
Average governability score	3	3	4	3.3	3.9	3.9	4.2	3.2	3.1

	EURO-CHAMBERS	EURO-CHLOR	EURO-COMMERCE	EUROFER	EURO-PABIO	EUROPIA/CONCAWE	EUROPE'S 500
Degree of specialism in the product chain		5	1	4	3	4	4
Issue-niche organisation		5	1	4	4	4	4
Member/non-member activity, in Brussels	1	3	1	1	2	2	
Counter-lobbying by members	2	4	2	2	2	3	
Involvement with cross-sectoral organisations		4	3	4	4	4	3
Specific regulatory regime activity/seeking		5	3	5	4	4	
Association used for lobbying	1	5	1	4	4	4	1
Association used for information	3	5	2	4	3	3	1
Prone to lowest common denominators	1	5	1	3	4	3	
Membership to avoid costs of non-membership	3	3	2	4	4	4	4
Membership for benefits of membership	1	5	1	4	4	4	4
Common enemy	2	5	5	2	5	4	
Collective cloak	3	5	1	2	5	4	
Extent of evaluation undertaken	2	5	3	5	3	4	2
Threat of exit	2	5	3	5	3	2	
EU identity in global trade		4	2	4	4	4	4
Degree of firms of similar size	2	3	1	5	2	4	
Membership density	2	4	2	5	4	4	
Overcapacity			3	5	2	4	
Extent of competition within sector		3	2	5	2	4	
Degree of concentration		4	2	4	3	4	
Disruptive merger & acquisitions activity			1	3	2	2	
Technology divisions					3	4	
Autonomy from members	3	3	1	4	3	2	3
Trust between members	3	4	1	4	3	4	
European or national markets		4	2	5	5	5	
Transaction-cost saving	3	5		4			
Other incentives, e.g. access to other organisations		4		4			
Average governability score	2.1	4.3	1.9	3.9	3.3	3.6	3

Table 4.1 Continued

	EUROPECHE	FAEP	FIEC	ORGALIME	UEAPME	UNICE
Degree of specialism in the product chain	4	4	3	2		
Issue-niche organisation	4	5	3	4		
Member/non-member activity, in Brussels	2	5	3	3	3	2
Counter-lobbying by members	1	4	3	3	3	2
Involvement with cross-sectoral organisations				4		
Specific regulatory regime activity/seeking	5	4	4	4		4
Association used for lobbying	1	4	3	2	5	3
Association used for information	1	4	3	5	5	2
Prone to lowest common denominators	1	3	2	3	4	5
Membership to avoid costs of non-membership	2	4	3	4	3	4
Membership for benefits of membership	1	3	3	4	5	4
Common enemy	2	3	3	4	4	5
Collective cloak	2	3	2	4	4	5
Extent of evaluation undertaken	3	3	3	4	4	5
Threat of exit	2	2	2	4	5	5
EU identity in global trade	4		3			5
Degree of firms of similar size	2	4	3	2	4	2
Membership density	2	3	2	4		3
Overcapacity	5	2				
Extent of competition within sector	3	2	2	2		
Degree of concentration	3	2	2	2		
Disruptive merger & acquisitions activity		3	4	3		
Technology divisions		2				
Autonomy from members	2	5	2	2	4	2
Trust between members	1	4	3	4	5	3
European or national markets	3	2	2	3	3	4
Transaction-cost saving				4		
Other incentives, e.g. access to other organisations	5					
Average governability score	2.5	3.3	2.7	3.3	4.1	3.6

Table 4.2 Variations in governability of EU business associations: weighted assessments

	ACE	ACEA	AEA	AIM	AMCHAM-EU	CAOBISCO	CBMC	CEA
Degree of specialism in the product chain	5	5	4	5		4	4	4
Issue-niche organisation	5	5	4	5		4	4	4
Member/non-member activity, in Brussels	3	1	2	2	2	3	3	3
Counter-lobbying by members	5	1	1	3	4	3	2	2
Involvement with cross-sectoral organisations	5			5			4	
Specific regulatory regime activity/seeking	5	3	4	4		5	5	3
Association used for lobbying	5	1	2	4	3	4	4	2
Association used for information	5	2	3	2	4	4	3	2
Prone to lowest common denominators	5	1	2	4		4	3	2
Membership to avoid costs of non-membership	5	1	4	3	4	4	4	4
Membership for benefits of membership	5	1	2	5	4	4	4	2
Common enemy	5	2	2	5	4	4	4	1
Collective cloak	5	2	2	4	5	4	2	1
Extent of evaluation undertaken	5	4	4	3	3	5	3	2
Threat of exit	5	4	4	2	3	5	3	2
EU identity in global trade	4	3	2			4	4	
Degree of firms of similar size	4	5	4	4	4	2	3	
Membership density						3	4	
Overcapacity	3	4	4	2		2	3	3
Extent of competition within sector	4	3	4	2		2	3	4
Degree of concentration	5	3	4	3		3	4	4
Disruptive merger & acquisitions activity	4	2	1				2	3
Technology divisions		2				3		
Autonomy from members		1	1	4	3	3	2	3
Trust between members		1	1	5	4	2	3	3
European or national markets	5	5	5	5	5	3		5
Transaction-cost saving								
Other incentives, e.g. access to other organisations								
Weighted average governability	4.7	2.6	2.9	3.7	3.7	3.5	3.3	2.8

Table 4.2 Continued

	CEFIC	CEMBUREAU	CEPS	CIAA	CIMSCEE	COCERAL	COLIPA	COPA/COGECA
Degree of specialism in the product chain	3	5	5	1	5	5	2	2
Issue-niche organisation	3	5	5	2	5	5	3	2
Member/non-member activity, in Brussels	2	4	2	2	2	4	3	1
Counter-lobbying by members	2	4	2	2	3	4	3	1
Involvement with cross-sectoral organisations	5	5	2	4	3	4	2	4
Specific regulatory regime activity/seeking	5	4	4	5	3	5	5	5
Association used for lobbying	4	5	2	4	2	4	4	3
Association used for information	5	5	3	4	3	4	5	3
Prone to lowest common denominators	3	4	3	1	4	4	4	1
Membership to avoid costs of non-membership	3	2	4	5	2	4	3	4
Membership for benefits of membership	5	5	2	3	4	4	5	1
Common enemy	5	5	4	4	1	5	5	4
Collective cloak	5	5	4	4	5	4	5	4
Extent of evaluation undertaken	5	5	4	4	5	5	3	4
Threat of exit	5	5	4	4	5	5	4	4
EU identity in global trade	2			5	5	5	4	2
Degree of firms of similar size	4	4	4	2	5	4	2	2
Membership density			4	3				
Overcapacity	4	5	4	2	4	4	3	4
Extent of competition within sector	4	5	4	3	4	4	2	3
Degree of concentration	4	5	2	3	3	3	2	3
Disruptive merger & acquisitions activity	2	4	3	3			2	
Technology divisions	3	3		3				
Autonomy from members	4	4	2	1	3	3	2	2
Trust between members	4	5	2	2	4	3	2	1
European or national markets	5	3	4	4	4	4	4	3
Transaction-cost saving	4							
Other incentives, e.g. access to other organisations	4					5		4
Weighted average governability	3.9	4.5	3.4	3.1	3.7	4.2	3.3	2.9

	CPIV	EAAA	EACEM	EAT	EBankU	EBroadcastingU	ECA	ECF
Degree of specialism in the product chain	5	5	3	2	3	4	5	4
Issue-niche organisation	5	5	3	5	4	5	5	4
Member/non-member activity, in Brussels	4	3	2	1	1	3	4	4
Counter-lobbying by members	2		2	2	1	4	4	3
Involvement with cross-sectoral organisations								
Specific regulatory regime activity/seeking	1	5	4	4	3	4	4	3
Association used for lobbying	3	4	4	1	3	4	5	4
Association used for information	3	4	3	1	2	4	4	4
Prone to lowest common denominators	2	4	2	3	1	4	3	3
Membership to avoid costs of non-membership	3	4	4	1	5	5	3	4
Membership for benefits of membership	3	4	3	2	2	5	3	4
Common enemy	4	4	3	2		3	4	2
Collective cloak	2	4	3	3		4		3
Extent of evaluation undertaken		5	2	2	1	5	3	4
Threat of exit	2	5	2	1	5	5	2	2
EU identity in global trade	1		4	4	3		5	4
Degree of firms of similar size	2	4	3	2	4	5	2	2
Membership density	2		2		4	5	2	3
Overcapacity		2	3				4	
Extent of competition within sector	2	2	4	3	2	4	4	3
Degree of concentration	2	4	2	4	2	5	2	4
Disruptive merger & acquisitions activity		2	2		2	5	3	4
Technology divisions			2	5	2		3	4
Autonomy from members	2	5	2	1	1	4	4	3
Trust between members	1	4	2	3	2	4	2	3
European or national markets	2	5	4	5			3	5
Transaction-cost saving							4	
Other incentives, e.g. access to other organisations								
Weighted average governability	2.5	4	2.9	2.5	2.5	4.3	3.5	3.5

Table 4.2 Continued

	ECSA	EDA	EEO	EFA	EFCA	EFPIA	EGTA	EMOTA
Degree of specialism in the product chain	4	3	5	4	5	4	4	3
Issue-niche organisation	4	3	5	4	5	4	4	4
Member/non-member activity, in Brussels	3	3	3	5	4	2	3	3
Counter-lobbying by members	2	3	3	4	3	2	3	3
Involvement with cross-sectoral organisations								
Specific regulatory regime activity/seeking	2	5	5	4	4	5	5	5
Association used for lobbying	4	3	5	2	3	4	5	4
Association used for information	4	3	4	1	3	3	5	4
Prone to lowest common denominators	4	2	3	2	3	3	3	4
Membership to avoid costs of non-membership	3	3	3	2	4	5	5	5
Membership for benefits of membership	4	3	5	1	3	4	5	4
Common enemy	4	3	5	2	3	4	4	4
Collective cloak	4	3	4			4	3	
Extent of evaluation undertaken	4	5	4	2	3	4	2	4
Threat of exit	4	4	2	2	1	5	2	4
EU identity in global trade	5	4			4		4	
Degree of firms of similar size	5	3	3	3	4	4	2	4
Membership density	5		2	2	2	5		
Overcapacity	5	4	2					
Extent of competition within sector	4	4	1	2	2	3	2	4
Degree of concentration	4	4	3	2	2	4	4	4
Disruptive merger & acquisitions activity						2	3	
Technology divisions	4		3					
Autonomy from members	4	3	4	3		3	3	3
Trust between members	4	3	3	2		4	1	4
European or national markets	5	3	4	1		5	3	2
Transaction-cost saving						4	4	5
Other incentives, e.g. access to other organisations								4
Weighted average governability	4	3.4	3.5	2.5	3.2	3.8	3.3	3.9

	ERT	ETRTO	EURATEX	EURELECTRIC	EUROCHAMBERS	EUROCHLOR
Degree of specialism in the product chain		5	2	2		5
Issue-niche organisation	5	5	2	2		5
Member/non-member activity, in Brussels	4	4	4	2	1	3
Counter-lobbying by members		4	3	2	2	4
Involvement with cross-sectoral organisations	4	4	4	5		5
Specific regulatory regime activity/seeking		2	4	3	1	5
Association used for lobbying		4	4	4	3	5
Association used for information		4	2	3	1	5
Prone to lowest common denominators	4	5	4	5	3	3
Membership to avoid costs of non-membership		4	4	3	1	5
Membership for benefits of membership	5	5	3	2		5
Common enemy		2	4	3	2	5
Collective cloak		1	3	4	3	5
Extent of evaluation undertaken	2	5	3	5	2	5
Threat of exit	3	5	5	1	2	5
EU identity in global trade	4	5	4	4		4
Degree of firms of similar size	5	5	3	4	2	3
Membership density		5	4	4	2	4
Overcapacity		5	2	3		
Extent of competition within sector		5	2	5		3
Degree of concentration		3		2		4
Disruptive merger & acquisitions activity						
Technology divisions	2	4	2			3
Autonomy from members	4	3	3	2	3	4
Trust between members	5	4	3	2	3	4
European or national markets		5	3	3		5
Transaction-cost saving		5			3	4
Other incentives, e.g. access to other organisations						
Weighted average governability	3.9	4.2	3.2	3.1	2.1	4.3

Table 4.2 Continued

	EURO-COMMERCE	EUROFER	EUROPE'S 500	EUROPABIO	EUROPIA/CONCAW
Degree of specialism in the product chain	1	4		3	4
Issue-niche organisation	1	4	4	4	4
Member/non-member activity, in Brussels	1	1	4	2	2
Counter-lobbying by members	1	2		2	3
Involvement with cross-sectoral organisations	2	4	3	4	4
Specific regulatory regime activity/seeking	3	5		4	4
Association used for lobbying	3	4	1	4	4
Association used for information	3	4	1	3	3
Prone to lowest common denominators	1	3		4	3
Membership to avoid costs of non-membership	2	4	4	4	4
Membership for benefits of membership	1	4	4	5	4
Common enemy	5	2		5	4
Collective cloak	1	2		3	4
Extent of evaluation undertaken	3	5		3	4
Threat of exit	3	5	2	4	4
EU identity in global trade	2	4		2	2
Degree of firms of similar size	1	5	4	4	4
Membership density	2	5		4	4
Overcapacity	3	5		2	4
Extent of competition within sector	2	5		2	4
Degree of concentration	2	4		3	4
Disruptive merger & acquisitions activity	1	3		2	2
Technology divisions				3	4
Autonomy from members	1	4	3	3	2
Trust between members	1	4		3	4
European or national markets	2	5		5	5
Transaction-cost saving		4			
Other incentives, e.g. access to other organisations		4			
Weighted average governability	1.9	3.9	3	3.3	3.6

	EUROPECHE	FAEP	FIEC	ORGALIME	UEAPME	UNICE
Degree of specialism in the product chain	4	4	3	2		
Issue-niche organisation	4	5	3	4		
Member/non-member activity, in Brussels	2	5	3	3	3	2
Counter-lobbying by members	1	4	3	3	3	2
Involvement with cross-sectoral organisations				4		
Specific regulatory regime activity/seeking	5	4	4	4	5	4
Association used for lobbying	1	4	3	2	5	3
Association used for information	1	4	3	5	5	2
Prone to lowest common denominators	1	3	2	3	4	5
Membership to avoid costs of non-membership	2	4	3	4	3	4
Membership for benefits of membership	1	3	3	4	5	5
Common enemy	2	3	3	4	4	5
Collective cloak	2	3	2	4	4	5
Extent of evaluation undertaken	3	3	3	4	4	5
Threat of exit	2	2	2	4	5	5
EU identity in global trade	4	4	3			5
Degree of firms of similar size	2	3	3	2	4	2
Membership density	2	2	2	4		3
Overcapacity	5	2				
Extent of competition within sector	3	2	2	2		
Degree of concentration	3	2	2	2		
Disruptive merger & acquisitions activity		3	4	3		
Technology divisions		2				
Autonomy from members	2	5	2	2	4	2
Trust between members	1	4	3	4	5	3
European or national markets	3	2	2	3	3	4
Transaction-cost saving				4		
Other incentives, e.g. access to other organisation	5					
Weighted average governability	2.5	3.3	2.7	3.3	4.1	3.6

and 'weighted' calculus (Table 4.2), with some small differences yielded by the weighting effect. Because these assess different things, the similarity in placing of associations between the two tables therefore provides some confidence in the results in that they are produced by different methods. Of the 49 associations, no association is more than five places different in ranking produced by the two methods (Table 4.3).

Table 4.3   Clusters of associations by simple and weighted variations

Simple average	Associability score	Weighted average	Associability score
ACE	4.7	CEMBUREAU	17.9
CEMBUREAU	4.5	ACE	17.6
EUROPEAN BROADCASTING UNION	4.3	EUROPEAN BROADCASTING UNION	16
EUROCHLOR	4.3	EAAA	15.7
ETRTO	4.2	EUROCHLOR	15.4
UEAPME	4.1	COCERAL	15.3
COCERAL	4.1	UEAPME	15.1
ECSA	4	ETRTO	14.9
EAAA	4	EMOTA	14.8
CEFIC	3.9	EUROFER	14.8
EMOTA	3.9	AIM	14.6
ERT	3.9	EFPIA	14.6
EUROFER	3.9	CEFIC	14.4
EFPIA	3.8	ECSA	14.4
AMCHAM-EU	3.7	ERT	14.1
AIM	3.7	AMCHAM-EU	13.8
CIMSCEE	3.7	CIMSCEE	13.7
EUROPIA	3.6	EEO	13.4
UNICE	3.6	EUROPIA	13.3
CAOBISCO	3.5	CAOBISCO	13.1
ECA	3.5	EGTA	13
ECF	3.5	EDA	12.8
EEO	3.5	CEPS	12.7
EGTA	3.3	ECF	12.5
EDA	3.4	UNICE	12.5
CBMC	3.3	ECA	12.2
CEPS	3.3	FAEP	12.2
COLIPA	3.3	CBMC	12
EUROPABIO	3.3	COLIPA	12
FAEP	3.3	EUROPABIO	12
ORGALIME	3.3	ORGALIME	12
EFCA	3.2	EURELECTRIC	11.9
EURATEX	3.2	EFCA	11.6

Table 4.3   Continued

Simple average	Associability score	Weighted average	Associability score
CIAA	3.1	CEA	11.5
EURELECTRIC	3.1	AEA	11.2
CEA	3	EURATEX	11.2
EUROPE'S 500	3	EUROPE'S 500	11.1
AEA	2.9	ACEA	10.7
COPA/COGECA	2.9	CIAA	10.6
EACEM	2.9	COPA/COGECA	10.5
CPIV	2.8	EACEM	10.4
FIEC	2.7	EFA	9.8
ACEA	2.6	CPIV	9.5
EAT	2.5	EAT	9.5
EUROPEAN BANKING UNION	2.5	FIEC	9.5
EFA	2.5	EUROPECHE	9.4
EUROPECHE	2.5	EUROPEAN BANKING UNION	9
EUROCHAMBRES	2.1	EUROCHAMBRES	7.5
EUROCOMMERCE	1.9	EUROCOMMERCE	7.3

This similarity enables the two indicators to be merged into one for some ease of analysis, through 'clustering' of impressions composited from each method. Clustering permits the assessment and comparison of the factors concerned between those in similar groups. It signifies, once again, the spirit in which the tables should be read. The table can be divided into four approximate cluster quartiles, and for more specialised analysis 10 approximate groups of five. In turn, this also allows an assessment of the weighting of factors.

FACTORS WEIGHTED '5'

From this group of factors, the most striking features concern the extent to which associations:

- with highly specialised missions are well-represented in the first cluster of five, while broad constituencies across the product chain are well-represented in the last cluster of five;
- with an 'autonomy' score of '4' or '5' are represented in the top quartile, while no association in the bottom quartile has an autonomy rating above 3;
- from domains where overcapacity issues are strongly present are well-represented in the first cluster quartile, while domains with a large number of

small operators are well-represented in the last cluster quartile. This factor is linked to the degree of concentration, in that a high degree of overcapacity leads to high industry concentration. Only one association appears in the lower quartile in which overcapacity issues are strongly present.

It is, however, possible that the prevalence of cases in the top-five placed associations with these factors strongly present is supported by the strength of presence of factors weighted '4'. Analysis of the results, however, does not suggest that this is the case.

Of the remaining factors with a '5' weighting there is a mixed picture. For instance, associations where the following factors are strongly present can be found among associations placed in both the top and the bottom quartile:

- a 'common enemy'
- a high degree of regulation
- a low threat of exit
- European markets

The strength of presence of each of these factors among associations in the lower quartile is either diluted by the absence or weak presence of other factors positively associated with governability, or the strong presence of other factors negatively associated with governability. Consequently, there is nothing in the results that challenges the weightings attributed to any one of the factors 'a common enemy', 'a high degree of regulation', 'a low threat of exit' or 'European markets'. What can be concluded, however, is that there appears to be a very strong association with governability for the concepts 'a high degree of specialisation', 'high autonomy' and (with a slight qualification) 'overcapacity/some degree of concentration'.

These indications can be supported by qualitative data from the interviews. Taking the issue of autonomy first, the absence of it in one association placed in the lowest quartile, together with the lack of trust between members (a '4' weighted factor), dominates the history of the association. This found expression in an agreement that the General Secretary of the association had to be recruited from outside of member companies. One of the main purposes of the association for its members appears to be to keep a watch on one another, and in particular to make sure that one member does not use the association as a vehicle of advantage through technical working standards that later form the basis for regulation. This association is one of the very few where almost all of its members run their own Brussels office. In these circumstances of low trust between members and low autonomy for the association, the 'cost of non-membership' factor is bound to be high, creating a high rationale for membership but a low degree of governability.

A contrary example is provided by a firm which had interests, for competitive reasons, in supporting opposing public interest groups in their quest to ban a key production process in which most members were involved, but did not do so because of longer-term trust issues, and the recognition of the potential need for collective action with those colleagues in the future. Reflecting on the importance of trust, one EU association General Secretary from a high technology product sector commented that:

> you have the people phenomenon ... when they start in the association they all hate each other ... you have to learn them how to work together ... when they meet 5/6 times they become colleagues in a common cause ... they help one another to do their jobs ... our members have to learn to work together.

Another EU association General Secretary, this time from an association in the agricultural supply chain, commented of their members that:

> people know each other well ... they can be the biggest competitors in the market ... when they come together they work extremely well together ... they have known each other for years.

This quotation indicates the importance of long-term relationships to the development of trust between members. Some associations have worked hard on trying to foster this quality though, as illustrated in earlier chapters, in some cases they have overdone it and ended up irritating members by building too much social time into meetings involving otherwise busy people. Where the balance is wrong, the association may be the subject of accusations that it is a tourism organisation.

Trust by the members in the personnel of the association, built up over a period of time, appears to be the key to the development of autonomy. One national association member commented of the EU General Secretary that:

> [he] is very good – and the autonomy he has earned works. He's been there for eight years, so he knows what the issues are. It really is people, and a question of the trust that you invest in the person doing the job for you to get it right, and confidence in them to know what divides us and to be aware of the differences.

High trust and autonomy may be linked to one of the other factors strongly associated with governability, a high degree of specialisation. Where specialisation is high, so members cannot avoid each other in the markets in which they operate, and the issues they seek to manage. Thus, trust may be a factor arising from iterative contact. Such a factor is evident between members of issue-specific associations, and in circumstances of high inter-member trust, so associations are likely to develop autonomy to undertake what they think is necessary on their behalf. It may also be fostered in cross-sectoral organisations, where the association is unlikely to be tied to the interests of one specific member and where the members are not necessarily in contact with one another in vertical product markets, but share a 'horizontal' interest.

Member trust can also arise from a high degree of concentration, and from overcapacity where members turn to associations to help them manage the over-capacity problem. Sometimes, trust can be too great in these circumstances, and the result can be temptations towards cartel-like behaviour. One EU association manager commented that:

> [this association] is regarded as a bit of a cartel by DG Competition. They would like large, concentrated players to be sharply fighting it out. They tend to be suspicious of associations.

These tendencies are present in at least a quarter of the first quartile cases. Where cartel-prone associations have exhibited a history of conflict between members in the courts – that is, where low trust is present – it is noticeable that the association concerned appears in the lowest quartile.

There was a lot of testimony from the interviews about the impact of a 'common enemy', whether this was perceived to be a public interest group, a labour market interest, a section of the political institutions, another interest in the product chain, or even (among associations of associations) non-member companies. Given this, it was a surprise to the author that the associations that appear to be seized by the 'common enemy' factor were highly dispersed throughout the quartiles. In the most clear-cut case in the first quartile, where members of an association have to buy time to enable the conversion of manufacturing plant, a very high degree of unity is provided by opposition on environmental grounds provided by a public interest group. In a case much lower down the quartiles, the reason for the lower placing was a low scoring on a number of other highly-rated factors. These included factors such as low trust between members, a history of personalised disputes between them, low associational autonomy, and a significant differentiation between firm size and thus interests in liberalisation or protectionism. In another case of a 'high common enemy' association, but placed low in the quartiles, the responsible factor once again seemed to be a differentiation between members along one main faultline, in this case between food and healthcare-type interests. Where the 'common enemy' is internal and only common to one specialism, so any perception of an enemy common to all is diluted.

There was some testimony to the importance of regulation, and the impact of the EU institutions upon associability. The strongest testimony to this came in sectors with a background of corporatist-type relations. For one association in the agricultural product chain, the Commission is clearly the 'glue' for the association; Commission consultative documents are sent only to the EU association, and membership of EU advisory committees is only available through the association. While these are now less important than they once were in agriculture, such committees still form an important part of policy-making (Gray, 1998), and pay the way for travel to Brussels. As the EU association General Secretary put it, 'they know exactly who will say what at the meetings ... it is a nice opportunity to see one another, and it pays the travel to Brussels'. This latter factor enables members to undertake other business, but even in the absence of this it provides a membership reason in its own right. Membership of an advisory body heightens self-esteem by the perception of being in a position to offer advice, sounds impressive to peers, provides a change from normal routines, offers respite from normal office demands and politics, and a chance to meet friends over a nice meal. If this latter factor and the common learning ground of the advisory committee enhances the ability of members to work together collectively through trust, shared understandings and value systems, so the association benefits. Where the association is the gatekeeper for these valued items, so the value of membership is clear.

Despite the general inability of EU institutions to provide the 'patronage' needed by associations, extensively discussed in Chapters 1 and 3, the preference of EU institutions for collective action was often cited by members in established, primary, sectors as a factor contributing to their continued associational membership. This factor appeared to be particularly prevalent in the agricultural and fisheries sectors, where there are historic traditions within EU institutions of working through EU associations, particularly in handing out advisory committee places only through the EU association, a role discussed below. However, although the preference of EU institutions for collective action has often been cited in general accounts of EU associability, it varies considerably. Although some members cited the EU institutions as a spur to collective action, the EU associations often saw the behaviour of the EU institutions as a hindrance to collective action. Exerpts taken from one annual report of an EU association record that:

> it was noted with great concern that certain Commissioners and senior Commission officials of importance to Orgalime have little or no regard for trade associations in any form (whether national or European) and turn to a selection of major companies directly for information and advice [p. 22] ... in view of the present negative attitude of some Commission personalities

towards most trade associations, and the special position some major companies have won as advisers to the senior echelons of the Commission. (Orgalime, 1996: 24)

Evidence from a small number of interviews conducted with officials from the EU institutions provide some confirmation for this. A deputy Director General saw federations as a particular problem, and commented to the author that:

We usually need to go deeper than the association of associations view ... they are seen as bureaucrats, not the people on the ground who know what they are talking about ... these are the people from firms. We need the practical view ... we structure the dialogue so we get the comments at one time ... Delors had this great fear of associations and the lowest common denominator problem ... we want to know what the real issues are, and talk to the people who have the real knowledge ... who are the people making the strategies of firms; who are the people able to change their minds if you argue with them ... these are the firms themselves ... We want the opinion leaders ... the behaviour leaders ... the practical people ... the constructive people ... not the recalcitrant (those against everything, negative about what business can do on this subject) ones to come alone ... we look for the progressive ones to take them forward. We are always trying to avoid lowest common denominators ... we try to be demanding. Often at these meetings we respond to industry ... we try to move it onwards to get them to do things for us. We try to get them to see things our way.

This account, once again, alludes to the key issue of autonomy among political representatives, with a preference for dialogue with those 'able to change their minds if you argue with them'. In this extremely rich quotation, the last sentence also stands out reminding the reader of the portrait painted by Grande (1996) of the Commission as a skilful operator with a clear view of what it is trying to achieve, in which it is the Commission that is doing the influencing of interest groups, and, if necessary, playing one interest off against another. Whilst this suggests that even those who participate are compromised, those interests that are unwilling or unable to play the game can be frozen out completely, and in consequence are unattractive to their members. Companies that participate with the Commission cannot be unaware of such views towards associations, although there is little evidence that it discourages them from collective action, perhaps for the wider range of reasons covered in Chapter 3 under the 'cost of non-membership' umbrella. However, it is something of an unexplained paradox that companies are exposed to these views of associations, and yet still prone to cite Commission preferences for collective action as a reason to participate in it.

In conclusion, the results obtained appear to justify the high weightings for each of the factors 'a common enemy', 'a high degree of regulation', 'a low threat of exit' and 'European markets'. However, there appears to be a very strong association with governability for the concepts 'a high degree of specialisation', 'high autonomy' and (with a slight qualification) 'overcapacity/some degree of concentration'.

FACTORS WEIGHTED '4'

Of the factors weighted '4', the importance of trust between members has already been highlighted. Of the other factors, the following summary observations arise from an analysis of Table 4.1 with 4.3:

- All of the associations placed in the lowest quartile for the unweighted placings received a score no greater than '2' for the factor 'prone to lowest common denominator' positions, with the exception of one association that did not receive a score for that factor. Similarly, all associations bar one in the top quartile for the unweighted placings received a score of '4' or above. Given the very strong relationship of this factor with governability, this provides some degree of confidence in the findings as a whole.
- Five of the associations in the lowest quartile had a ranking of '4' or above for the factor 'firms of similar size', emphasising that this condition is not sufficiently strong on its own to ease governability.
- Few associations had members who undertook a significant degree of 'evaluation', such that the factor could not be one of variation between associations.
- Most associations scored highly on the 'cost of non-membership' factor, so once again it is difficult to use it as a factor of variation. However, associations scoring highly on the 'costs of non-membership' factor and more than two scores lower on the 'benefits of membership' factor tended to be among the lower quartiles. Only two of the 13 associations obtaining a '5' rating on the 'benefits of membership' factor were not included in the top quartile in either the simple, or weighted, average clusters. This is indicative of the discussion about low autonomy and trust above – that is, that where members use the association principally on the grounds of the 'cost of non-membership', there may be a low degree of governability.
- Only one of the 12 associations scoring highly – '4' or above – on the factor 'counter-lobbying by members' factor (that is low degree of counter-lobbying by members) appears outside the top quartile in either the simple, or weighted, average clusters. Similarly, just two of the organisations in the

lowest quartiles had a score higher than '2' on this rating. This confirms the association with governability that might be expected of this factor.

These summary observations are confirmed by the qualitative evidence. The greatest richness of these referred to the lack of evaluation of membership, the extent to which associability is normal behaviour, and the related though slightly different cost of non-membership factor. Despite substantial criticisms among the members of some associations placed in the lowest quartile, there was no question of exit, despite annual affiliation fees of up to € half a million among this cluster. A public affairs manager of a large US–German multinational commented that:

> it is a natural reaction and instinct in Europe to join your association, and you don't ask why. In Europe the question is rather 'why do you leave it?' than 'why do you join it?'.

Similarly, another public affairs manager for a French-based multinational responded to a question about why his company was a member of the EU business association in question, with the comment:

> the habits, why not? Shouldn't the question be 'why not?' It is just normal behaviour, just what we do. Not to join is not normal behaviour. We do not like to be considered apart from a majority of the companies. It is just the thing to do.

From the same sector, a public affairs manager for a US multinational confirmed the lack of evaluation of membership, but focused less on 'habit' and more on the 'cost of non-membership' factor. Responding to a question about evaluation of membership, he replied:

> Do we evaluate on a cost/benefit basis? Largely not – it is balancing the collective cloak versus our position on an issue. You will have to compromise ... the collective cloak is the greatest benefit, but you have to look to the bottom line of whether the trade association benefit is good enough for you. On balance the collective cloak is the strongest. Anyway, if you are not a member you have no influence whatsoever if you are not inside. You can never quantify this ... hence we do not really do a cost/benefit calculation.

These two replies, from the same sector, indicate the difficulties of coming to conclusions about sectoral characteristics driving variation. Nonetheless, even across sectors there was very little evidence of evaluation. From a national association in a large firm financial services sector, a General Secretary commented that:

> We don't calculate the cost or benefits of being a member of the [EU association]. We are a member, because we feel we should be a member. We are an important [sector] association and there is a pan-European association for us, so we are a member. The reason for membership is not because of costs and benefits.

A member of this association commented that: 'no one even thinks about membership. Our membership is on auto pilot. It is protocol that you are a member'. Another association manager, this time in the chemical sector, commented that:

> you cannot just have trade association membership when you need it. We do no cost/benefit analysis. In theory it is nice to have it, but you just cannot do without it. You have to be practical. For our sector associations, leaving just does not arise. It is just not a question.

These comments were quite typical of national association managers, whose *raison d'être* is collective action. One commented that:

> We believe in collective action. You're more powerful if you act together. This is why [Swedish association] exists and it would be odd if we didn't have the same philosophy when it comes to the EU. It is not that we have to hide ourselves. When organisations with common interests come together we should be one of them. It would be against our basic philosophy not to participate. It's natural.

'Free-riding' of EU associations does not appear to be an option for either national associations or for large firms. A large firm in the courier sector commented that:

> if you are the largest in the world you accept that there will be free riders. We are going to benefit most from a global trade liberalisation ... it will be more for us than the smaller ones ... so we are prepared.

Whilst this rather challenges Olsonian explanations of collective action, there is also evidence for collective action arising from mechanisms of peer pressure envisaged by Olson. One General Secretary of an EU association which had recently admitted firms alongside national association members in response to the increasing presence of large companies in the sector in Brussels, commented that 'there is a peer pressure thing ... the atmosphere from the companies is to run with it'. Additionally, iterative member interaction may contribute to shared understandings, and trust, in the manner described above. Consequently, the presence of a member in Brussels, a '3'-weighted factor discussed below, may assist with associational governability as well as threatening it.

In conclusion, of the group of factors weighted 4, the results obtained generate some confidence in the findings and provide some justification for the weightings. The exception to this was for the factor 'firms of similar size', which does not stand alone as a sufficient indicator of governability. As expected, there is a strong relationship between a high degree of counter-lobbying by members and low governability. Perhaps of greatest interest from this set of factors concerns the 'cost of non-membership' versus 'benefits of membership' nexus. On its own, the cost of non-membership type of issues appears to be an insufficient predictor of governability, unless it is coupled with the benefits of membership perception. Yet there is very little evaluation of the benefits of membership set against the costs because membership appears to arise from 'habit' or 'auto-pilot'-type behaviour. In particular, membership seems to be regarded as normal political behaviour, largely because EU associations were established for the purposes of political representation by organisations that were themselves politically active in the first instance.

FACTORS WEIGHTED '3'

Many of these factors provide confirmatory evidence for factors in higher-weighted categories, or yielded tentative conclusions on the grounds of low numbers:

- Three factors in this group could not be assessed for all, or even most, associations, because of a limited amount of available information. However, of those that could, organisations that received a '5' score for each of the factors 'transaction-cost savings', 'membership density' and 'involvement with cross-sectoral organisations' were almost invariably placed in the top quartile. A higher rating for these factors is almost certainly justified. Amongst the illustrative comments of the importance of transaction-cost savings, one national association talked about the importance of managing some of these costs for their members:

  the biggest issue in this sector is how can you cut your costs of doing business and in Ireland it is very difficult to do this because of the abolition of PRSI (Pay Related Social Insurance) ceiling, the difficulty in employing people, transport costs in relation to what it costs in relation to a sister company operating in the UK, and the distribution costs which are massive on account of such poor infrastructure.

- Unsurprisingly, the factor 'issue niche organisation' displayed characteristics similar to that of the '5'-weighted factor 'degree of specialism in the product chain', and may therefore have justified a similar weighting.
- The majority of associations scoring a '5' on the factor 'association used for lobbying' appeared in the top quartile, whereas all of those scoring a '1' for this factor appeared in the lowest quartile. Again unsurprisingly, the scoring for this factor was similar to that of the '4'-weighted factor 'membership for 'benefits of membership,' providing useful confirmatory evidence to the discussion above.
- Only one of the seven associations scoring a '1' on the factor 'member/non-member activity in Brussels' (that is, a high degree of activity) appeared outside of the lowest quartile. There is a difference in concept between this factor and the factor 'counter-lobbying by members', in that it is possible for members to be in Brussels without undertaking a significant counter-lobbying role. Similarly, a counter-lobbying role can be undertaken from the member states, given the multiple access points to Brussels politics. Whilst the results do indicate some differences between these factors, the similarities are greater than the differences. Whilst members based in Brussels may play more or less supportive roles to their associations, it is difficult to imagine that investment in a Brussels base and full-time staff bears no relation to counter-lobbying activity.

By conclusion, many of the factors weighted '3' were related to others in a higher weighting category. Of these, associations presenting their members with 'transaction-cost savings' demonstrated a relationship with governability. So too did the factors 'issue-niche organisations', and 'association used for lobbying', although these were more 'son of' rather than 'parent' factors. Those which presented a strong independent association with governability tended to be those which were either restricted to a small number of associations, such as 'involvement with cross-sectoral associations', or about which limited information was available, such as 'membership density'.

FACTORS WEIGHTED '2'

- All associations in the top quartile bar one received a score of '4' (six associations) or '5' (five associations) for the factor 'association used for information'. Half of all associations in the lowest quartile received a score of '1' or '2'.

Whilst there is a relationship between this score and governability, it is less clear cut than the 'family' factors to which it belongs, 'membership for benefits of membership', and 'membership for costs of non-membership'. As discussed in Chapter 3, the availability of information about EU-related matters through media like the world wide web mean that members now have a greater ability to access the formal information sources they need for themselves, thereby reducing their dependence upon the association. Many members also commented on how their associations generate too much information for them to sift through, partly to protect themselves from charges of dereliction of duty in case a particular issue flares up later. Nonetheless, associations and the meeting opportunities they provide are one source of formal and of 'informal' information (gossip, rumours, intelligence), and thus a benefit of membership. Even if this benefit has not recently been evident, the cost of non-membership is potentially high in that loss of access to information that might prove vital at a future point could be costly. The mean score of 3.4 for this factor across the 48 associations rated on this factor reflects these considerations.

- There was a tendency for the factor 'extent of competition within a sector' to behave similarly to the factor 'overcapacity', discussed in the '5'-weighted factors above. In general, high overcapacity means low competition, and vice versa. Only two cases were more than one score apart, in domains where there is high overcapacity but also relatively high competition. The nature of these domains has made them unsuitable for concentration into large firms, and each are characterised by a relatively high number of long-established, small and medium-sized businesses, in one case a primary sector tied to communities with specific geographical features. In general, however, the results obtained suggest that the factor might have obtained a higher rating.

- There was sometimes only limited information with which to assess associations by the extent to which their domains have been subject to disruptive 'mergers and acquisitions activity'. Of those in the highest quartile, more organisations received a low scoring than a high one. Of the seven organisations rated in the lowest quartile, most received a '2'.

- Just 14 associations were rated on the factor 'technology divisions', and just one of these score at the extremes ('5' or '1'). From this group of associations, little could be established about the importance of this factor to governability.

- Just seven associations were rated on the 'other incentives, e.g. access to other organisations'. All of these, however, received a rating of '4' or '5'. All bar one of these associations were in domains representing primary, and/or very mature, activities. The EU associations concerned were long-established, and date from an era where EU policy-making was dominated by advisory committees, with access to them provided solely by the EU association. In one case this provided the principle *raison d'être* for the association in a sector where collective action on a European level is otherwise extremely difficult for competitive reasons.

By conclusion, of these factors, on the whole the weighting of '2' appears justified. In the main, other factors did not yield strong signals, or were strongly linked to other factors. The one factor to stand out on its own, 'access to other organisations', was a relatively rare phenomenon, but where it did arise it had a positive impact upon governability.

FACTORS WEIGHTED '1'

- Whilst associations frequently refer to the importance of a 'collective cloak' in sustaining the organisation in general terms, the question asked in this survey related to a very specific need for members to use the identity of the association when particularly controversial issues pressed. On this issue, the top quartile cluster mostly scored '4', with three '5' scores, and just one with a score of '1'. Thus, the presence of the factor tended to be included within the profile of associations with a high degree of governability. A national association commented that:

  > I suppose for a lot of our members they deliberately choose to be a member of an association in terms of their European relationships because for some much larger companies they don't want to be seen as acting alone if they are lobbying the government on something that may be a quite contentious issue and may not be seen by the general public as ethical. They don't want to be seen as company A, which is pro giving alcohol to children for example. It is easier for them, and they can achieve a lot more, if they are a member of an association.

  Whilst the presence of a highly controversial issue might be included among the portfolio of associations with a high profile of governability, it should not in itself be equated with a high degree of governability. Hence, the distribution of scores for this factor is a little different from that of the related factor, a 'common enemy', and in a deductive sense a 'common enemy' need not be a controversial issue requiring a 'collective cloak'. Only where the issue is both controversial and an enemy in common to virtually all of the constituency or members is the factor likely to promote cohesion among members.
- Five of the seven associations scoring a '5' on the factor 'EU identity in global trade' were outside of the top quartile, indicating that the presence of

this condition alone is not a strong predictor of governability. Of the two that were not, one was an organisation primarily used for technical product standards, which were used by members as the basis for competitive advantage by seeking to 'export' these in the hope of getting them adopted as global standards. As described in Chapter 3, this concept was also used by members for defensive reasons in the product chain.

In conclusion, the presence of these factors may contribute to governability, but by themselves they are not a condition for it. The '1' weighting appears to be justified for these factors.

REVIEW OF WEIGHTINGS

The position of the associations in the top, and bottom quartiles of the simple average placings in the main justify the weightings attached to the factors. The exception to this is the variable 'firms of similar size', where associations that scored highly on this factor were to be found in the top, and lowest, quartiles. Most of the variables with some degree of independence, that is causal factors, are concentrated in the factors weighted '4' and '5'. Of the factors originally weighted below '4', a small number indicated some degree of independence, although most of these were specialised factors against which few associations could be rated. Of this latter group 'access to other organisation' and 'involvement with cross-sectoral association' appear to be factors that justify a higher rating on the basis of the limited evidence presented. Of all factors, the strongest association with governability appears for the factors 'a high degree of specialisation', 'high autonomy' and (with a slight qualification) 'overcapacity' in conjunction with a relatively 'high degree of concentration'. These three factors might receive a special weighting in any future study.

The results also indicated the extent to which factors were related. 'Families' of closely related factors appear to be:

- Overcapacity, the degree of competition, and the extent of concentration within a sector, where the presence of high overcapacity coupled with a low degree of competition and a relatively high degree of concentration appears to be justified for treatment as a highly significant independent variable.
- The cost of non-membership, but only in conjunction with the benefits of membership and related factors such as the use of the association for lobbying, or a low degree of counter-lobbying. Somewhere in between these also fits the factor 'low threat of exit'. Again, the presence of these factors together appears to justify their treatment as a significant independent variable.

- The degree of specialism, together with issue-niche organisations – each very strongly associated with governability, with one a subset of the other rather than combination factors.

Analysis was undertaken of the average scores received for each factor for the sample of associations (Table 4.4). As a measure of variation, a standard deviation (SD) of 0.48 from a mean score of 3.4 (SD) indicates variability in scores between the factors that are by no means extreme or in any way unusual, but which at the same time indicates variability of significance. Whilst some caution should be

Table 4.4   Average associational score per factor

Factor*	Average associational score
Degree of specialism in the product chain	3.9
Issue-niche organisation	4.1
Member/non-member activity in Brussels	2.7
Counter-lobbying by members	2.7
Involvement with cross-sectoral organisations	4
Specific regulatory regime activity/seeking	4.2
Association used for lobbying	3.4
Association used for information	3.4
Prone to lowest common denominators	2.9
Membership to avoid costs of non-membership	3.7
Membership for benefits of membership	3.5
Common enemy	3.5
Collective cloak	3.4
Extent of evaluation undertaken	3.7
Threat of exit	3.5
EU identity in global trade	3.6
Degree of firms of similar size	3.5
Membership density	3.2
Overcapacity	3.5
Extent of competition within sector	3
Degree of concentration	3.3
Disruptive merger & acquisitions activity	2.5
Technology divisions	3.3
Autonomy from members	2.7
Trust between members	3
European or national markets	3.8
Transaction-cost saving	4.1
Other incentives, e.g. access to other organisations	4.3
Average score	3.4

* See Table 3.1 for an indication of the association of factors with governability.

exercised in respect of averages for those factors with a low number of scores allocated, such as 'other incentives' (6), 'transaction-cost saving' (11), 'technology divisions' (14) and 'involvement with cross-sectoral organisations' (14), the average number of associations to be rated against each factor was 39, representing 79 per cent of all possible assessments. Some degree of confidence in the results is given by the similar scores obtained for cognate factors, such as 'specialism' (3.9) and 'issue niche' (4.1), 'member activity' and 'counter-lobbying in Brussels' (both 2.7), 'overcapacity' (3.5) and 'degree of concentration' (3.3).

For the individual factors, this sample of associations displayed a governability score of 4 or above on the issues of 'regulation', 'specialism' (issue niche and specialism combined), 'transaction-cost savings' and 'other incentives'. Because two of these factors had a low number of ratings, some caution should be expressed with these, although it might reasonably be concluded that where these factors present themselves, they have a significant impact upon governability. Factors where associations obtained an average governability score below 3 include 'the degree of autonomy from members', the 'extent of counter-lobbying by members', and the 'degree of member and non-member activity' in Brussels. There is nothing in these results to challenge the weightings allocated to the factors, though they do provide some interesting indications about this sample of EU business associations. In general, the associations in this sample had a low degree of autonomy, a high degree of counter-lobbying by members, and a high degree of specialisation. These three factors are linked, and help paint a picture. The lack of patronage of EU institutions provides for the triumph of the logic of membership over the logic of influence, in that specialisation is the main source of coherence in the absence of patronage. This specialisation leads to low membership numbers and associations that are closely controlled by their members, and which consequently lack autonomy. Associations that are closely controlled by their members are unable to add value for them, leading to members undertaking their own lobbying activities. There are other linkages between these factors, such as the lack of ability for EU institutions to provide patronage for EU associations providing a stimulus for high degrees of counter-lobbying.

5 Business-Wide Associations

In this chapter, descriptions are provided of the business-wide associations AMCHAM-EU (EU Committee of the American Chamber of Commerce), ERT (European Round Table of Industrialists), EUROCHAMBRES (Association of European Chambers of Commerce and Industry), UEAPME (European Association of Craft, Small and Medium-Sized Enterprises) and UNICE (Union of Industrial and Employers' Confederations of Europe), followed by an assessment of the 'governability' of each of these organisations drawn both from the wider literature in the public domain and from the results presented in Chapter 4. The wider literature was used alongside survey factors to assess governability because some of the factors of governability are more oriented towards sectoral organisations and could not be used for cross-sectoral organisations. Thus, indicators of governability that could not be used included the degree of presence of (weighting in brackets):

- specialism in the product chain (5);
- an issue-niche organisation (3);
- involvement with cross-sectoral organisations (3);
- a specific regulatory regime (5);
- an overcapacity problem (5);
- concentration (4);
- disruptive merger and acquisitions activity (2);
- technology divisions (2).

In addition, some other factors are very difficult to apply, such as transaction-cost savings, and access to other organisations, because these are more applicable to the narrower circumstances in which domain-based associations operate, such as information collection for product-specific contexts, or access to standards institutes. Business-wide associations do less of these things than do domain-specific associations, although they may arise in some format, such as generally applicable lower costs arising from restricting the cost of employment or environmental legislation. At the end of this chapter, a revised typology of factors is developed and applied for business-wide associations.

Consequently, the positions of these organisations among the rankings presented in Chapter 4 should be taken with some caution, as assessments were not made for between one-quarter and one-third of the factors. Thus, the organisation with the biggest difference in placing between the simple and weighted assessments was UNICE, dropping six places amongst the weighted average placings. In addition, an issue which is outlined in greater depth below is the special position of the ERT, and the difficulty of applying criteria of governability to an organisation which is quite different in concept from all of the other business-wide representative organisations. Indeed, ERT does not seek to represent a business-wide constituency, but draws its members from a select group of large firms. For all these reasons, much greater caution should be exercised in using the indicators from the survey of governability in the case of business-wide associations than in the case of sectoral organisations.

Business-wide organisations have advantages and disadvantages of governability when compared to sectoral organisations. Certainly, the size of constituency they represent makes coming to common positions difficult, and there may be a natural tendency towards 'lowest-common-denominator' positions. Nonetheless, as these organisations are not tied to the interests of one specific constituency, sector or interest, but rather represent a diversity of constituencies, they tend to operate with greater autonomy than do sector-specific organisations. As described in Chapter 1, each of these organisations is in some way limited in its embrace, in that there is no organisation with a constituency embracing all business regardless of territory (Europe; non-Europe), format (association of firms, or association of associations) or size (large, medium, small).

Another major factor of difference between business-wide and domain-specific associations is that some of the former are endowed with functions as employer associations. Business-wide employer associations are deeply motivated in their formation and development by worker organisation through trade unions. All of the associations reviewed in this chapter comment on generally applicable employment measures, and in this sense there are different dynamics at work with members and potential members. However, it is important to qualify this. A much smaller number of them are endowed with capacities and mandates to engage trade union organisations. There is no EU-wide business organisation with a general mandate from its members to engage in collective bargaining, and indeed the architecture, powers of and structure of interests in the EU make it difficult to imagine collective bargaining as we know it at the national level emerging at the EU level. Consequently, no EU-wide business association possesses the kinds of capacities to discipline members that exist at the national level, and there is therefore a major limit imposed on the development and governance capacities of EU associations in consequence. Instead of EU-level collective bargaining, the nearest cousin involves policy-making capacities endowed through EU social partnership arrangements. Nonetheless, the function of social partnership does have an impact upon member–association dynamics in the case of UNICE and UEAPME, the two business-wide EU associations which fully participate in these, and, in a much more restricted sense, upon EUROCHAMBRES. These are commented on in the chapter below, although the general extent of the impact of social partnership upon EU business associations is summarised here first.

It is worth starting first with observations as to the limits of social partnership upon mechanisms of governability in EU business associations. Both UNICE and UEAPME need to seek a fresh, issue-specific mandate from their members to engage in the process. The rules of each of these associations mean that neither of them have capacities to exercise authority over their members in this process, or to bind members against their will. None of the other organisations surveyed in this chapter have any sort of a mandate from their members to engage trade unions in formal procedures and to come to collective agreements. There is a sense in which this general lack of endowment of EU business associations is a source of strength for business more generally, in that business interests are not drawn into making agreements they do not like. This paradox is, however, of greatest impact in a historic sense, when it made sense for business interests to make sure that their representative organisations did not become drawn into making collective agreements with trade unions. There are obligations imposed by the EU social partnership procedures. UNICE inevitably become drawn into the process after a pragmatic realisation that it would be in a better position to pursue the interests of business from the inside. This followed on from the ability of the Commission to be in a position to be able to say 'negotiate or we'll legislate' after it became clear that QMV in the social field would be extended (see Branch and Greenwood, 2001). Later, when UNICE had signed up to the procedures, UEAPME successfully realised its ambition to be included. In this sense, both of these organisations have assumed an importance in the EU policy process, and the importance of them to their members has taken on a different form. In the past, the task for members was to try to ensure that their representative organisations did not become engaged in anything resembling collective bargaining. Now that this has become inevitable, it has generated a more active involvement by members on an issue by issue basis. Either way, these rationales alone make it hardly imaginable that any member might have taken the decision to exit from organisations such as UNICE or UEAPME. A final observation is the development of the social dialogue at the sectoral level. Whilst this does not resemble the legislative capacities of social partnership involving the cross-business organisations, it is worth noting that it has been used as a recruiting sergeant by associations at the sectoral level. Undoubtedly, the development of sectoral social dialogue will have an impact upon the dynamics of sectoral business associations in the years to come.

A final point, prior to looking at each of the organisations in depth, is to consider the types of organisations they are. UNICE, UEAPME and ERT are not in any way service providers; they exist purely for the purpose of engaging in EU politics. AMCHAM-EU primarily does this too, although it is a member-driven organisation with substantial member services. The strength of EUROCHAMBRES is much more as a network and a service provider than a political representative, although it seeks to undertake this function too. These organisations are much more in the public domain, as business-wide organisations engaging 'high' politics as well as technical concerns of low politics, and a good deal of information is available about them from a variety of public sources. For this reason there are less sensitivities attached to them, and organisations are described individually rather than the more general treatment of sectoral (domain-specific) organisations in Chapter 4. Consistent with the title of this book, this chapter seeks to go 'inside' these business-wide associations. As UNICE is the closest to an all-embracing business association, with employer functions, this organisation is described first and at greatest length.

UNICE

Formed in 1958, the Union of Industrial and Employers' Confederations of Europe now has 33 full members, these being national associations of business from 26 countries spread geographically from Iceland to Turkey, Norway to Malta, and Finland to Portugal. Among these 26 countries are included associations from each of the EU member states, including the main contributor countries of France, Germany, Italy and the UK.[1] There are also a number of members from EFTA and the applicant countries, joined by observers from five other applicant or would-be countries. With the debatable exception of Austria,[2] these associations represent the most significant business-wide organisations in each of these countries. Hence, UNICE claims to represent 'the vast majority of 17 million SMEs and large businesses active in Europe' (Institut des Sciences du Travail (IST), 1999).

Almost three-quarters of UNICE members (24) have offices in Brussels, including many with offices in the same building complex as UNICE. These supplement the work of the 48 staff members of UNICE, and much of their work

---

[1] These four countries each contribute 13% of the annual budget, followed by Spain (7.48%, the Netherlands (6.9%), Belgium (6.27%), Sweden (5.234%), Denmark (4.4%), Austria (2%) through to Portugal at 1.2% and Luxembourg at 0.3%).

[2] The Austrian member of UNICE is the Association of Austrian Industrialists, the VÖI, representing private sector companies, rather than the larger Austrian Federal Economic Chamber, the WKÖ, representing private and public companies. UNICE excludes the WKÖ from membership on the grounds that it regards the WKÖ as insufficiently independent from the machinery of Austrian government. The WKÖ is instead a member of UEAPME, where its size (250000 members) and position makes it a powerful member. The situation is thus an exception arising from the highly corporatist nature of Austrian economic governance.

is highly coordinated with UNICE, including the presentation of UNICE positions to national MEPs. Thus, the resources they bring and the support they offer is central to the work of UNICE. There has been insufficient emphasis given in analyses of the organisation to the dependence of UNICE upon the quality of its relationships with, and between, these member offices. This is a factor that can also be overlooked among those new to the UNICE secretariat, even amongst those in relatively senior positions, in that the top member officials in the member states who may have scant knowledge of UNICE's concerns rely upon their Brussels offices for their impressions of the organisation, briefings and as a basis of decision-taking. Going over the heads of permanent delegates, in particular, has led to longer-term problems. UNICE staff present in post for any length of time come to appreciate that relationships with member offices in Brussels are important influences upon their own effectiveness, and take some time to cultivate these relationships. This can then become reflected in the seniority of staff sent by members as permanent delegates, and the length of time they remain in post. In turn, this longevity, together with the simple presence of so many of these offices in Brussels, can assist with building the key quality of intra-member trust and helps UNICE to explain the association to the members. Members can see, assess and come to share a problem if they are on the spot and appreciate how difficult it is to find a solution, rather than demanding one from a remote base regardless of the difficulties. In short, the permanent member offices in Brussels are a key mechanism to consensus building.

Much has been made of the supportive role of the Brussels offices of national members. They are close to nationals from their own country who work in the Commission, the Parliament, COREPER and in the Council. Through these contacts they can obtain virtually any document, and ensure that UNICE positions are known to the people that matter. However, these contacts can also be a dual-edged sword. The offices are also independent entities, and while the balance of their contribution to UNICE is supportive, it would be naive to think that they do not undertake their own lobbying activities when the positions of their patrons differ from those of UNICE over matters of some importance to them. Another counterside to these offices is that their proximity to the UNICE secretariat has the potential to restrict the autonomy of the latter through increased monitoring. This is reflected in the mandate of the Unice Committee of Permanent Delegates, a sub-committee of the Executive Committee based around the national-member Brussels delegations.[3] This organisation is charged with 'the selection of issues to be dealt with and the organisation of work in their regard, as well as the day to

---

[3] The smaller members that do not have an office in Brussels (e.g. Luxembourg, San Marino, Cyprus and some of the Central and East European members) are mailed papers, and occasionally attend these meetings.

day representation of the associations' (Institut des Sciences du Travail, 1999). To reflect this operational mandate, the committee meets every two weeks.

The task of UNICE is to defend and promote the interests of its members *vis-à-vis* the institutions of the EU. Because any organisation with such a wide membership constituency is bound to have some difficulties in reaching common positions, it is something of a cheap point to be critical of it on the basis of a tendency towards lowest-common-denominator positions. Its former General Secretary, Zygmunt Tyszkiewicz, presents the other side of this equation, referring instead to the 'miracle' of its cohesiveness under the circumstances of its breadth of membership constituency (Tyszkiewicz, 2001). The 'miracle' interpretation is a balanced counter to a view presented by an unnamed 'former senior EU official' in a recent *Financial Times* article, who is quoted as saying that:

> Unice's problem is that it consists of a federation of confederations. It is a heavily bureaucratic system, even though it is the only recognised body that represents formally the whole of European industry. In short, it is a reactive institution whereas the ERT with its minimal bureaucracy is proactive. (Betts, 2001)

Whilst there is a ring of truth about some of this, the quote should not be taken out of context. It fails to recognise that UNICE is a completely different animal to ERT. UNICE seeks to defend the broad interests of the entire constituency of European business in everyday public affairs, based around national representative business-wide associations, whereas the ERT draws from a strictly selected membership of invited CEOs from large (mainly manufacturing) companies and performs a 'strategic-issue think-tank' role. Certainly, UNICE was at a low point at the time of the creation of the ERT in 1983, though as discussed below the relationship between these factors was not causal. The organisation was somewhat overhauled following the appointment of Tyszkiewicz, who became its longest serving General Secretary by holding the post from 1985 to 1998. A good deal of the credit for turning the organisation into a lively and dynamic centre of business representation belongs to him, including the creation of the UNICE Advisory and Support Group (UASG), described and analysed in Chapter 1. For the record, the members of this organisation as of 1998 are recorded in Table 5.1.

Whilst UNICE does have something of an elegant diplomacy culture which is not dissimilar from some national civil services, this is a reflection of the breadth of interests it embraces. This breadth can be a source of strength for UNICE as well as a weakness. It allows the organisation to speak with some authority based on the extent of its constituency, and it has also allowed UNICE to be incorporated under the EU Treaties into EU decision-making through its

Table 5.1 Members of the UNICE
Advisory and Support Group, 1998

Bayer AG
BP Europe
Compania Sevillana de Electicidad
Dow Europe
Esso Coordination Center n.v.
Exxon Company International
Diageo
Hydro S.A.
IBM Europe
ICI
Iveco SpA
KONE International S.A.
Lyonnaise des Eaux
Mars Confectionery
Michelin
Mondial International
Norsk Hydro A.S.
Philip Morris
Procter & Gamble
Shell
Solvay
The Coca-Cola Company
Time Warner Europe Inc
Unilever NV
VEBA AG

---

role as a designated 'social partner'. Through this, it is empowered to work with other 'social partners' from business, the public sector and trade unions to reach agreement on labour market issues and forward the text of its agreement directly to the Council of Ministers for candidate adoption as a European Directive. In this role, it pragmatically exerts the interests of business in shaping, or declining to shape, EU social legislation (see Branch and Greenwood, 2001). This now forms one of the two central missions of UNICE alongside general industry representation work, and this institutionalised role in EU policy-making, provided since the 1992 Treaty on European Union, has helped to maintain its status at the centre of EU business interest representation.

Another widely recognised feature of the breadth of UNICE's constituency is that decision-making can be lengthy as members need to consult with their own extensive memberships. Longevity in reaching decisions is a feature of all representative organisations with an active constituency, although almost all have a fast-track decision-making procedure for emergency situations where necessary.

Where the membership constituency is less active, so decision-making is speeded up because the consultative routines are lighter. This factor may make associations representing small-business constituencies nimbler on their feet. It also provides an advantage for organisations representing highly fragmented constituencies based on individuals, such as public interest groups, where there are no real prospects for consultation. In these circumstances an association is relatively free to reach decisions quickly, and come to highly focused policy positions that have not been subjected to extensive compromise. UNICE is the structural opposite of this in representing national associations of business, because the positions of these associations as established players in national politics are in turn closely contested by their own members. Consultation therefore takes time.

At the end of 1999, the UNICE Council of Presidents attempted to alleviate this structural difficulty by the introduction of qualified majority voting (QMV). Though voting is seldom used, the spectre of QMV has speeded up reaction times. The Council of Presidents, comprising the Presidents of the member federations, is the supreme decision-making body. Apart from constitutional powers of amending statutes, electing the President and admitting new members, this tier receives the outcomes of social partner negotiations for approval, and considers any matters that have not been resolved in the Executive Committee. The Rules of Procedure lean towards caution, in that they determine 'should the Executive Committee not be able to adopt a position paper unanimously, *any member* of the Committee may ask for the matter to be referred to the Council' (my emphasis) (UNICE, 1997: 5[4]). This emphasis upon consensus, and carrying all members with the organisation on each position, is evident throughout the culture of the organisation. This culture should be expected of an organisation whose principal strength is its breadth of representativity. The Statutes record that 'in adopting a position, the Association shall *normally* seek a consensus among its members' (my emphasis) (*ibid.*: 6[5]). There is inevitably a trade-off in longer decision-taking times. Before the introduction of QMV in 1999, the same article continues by recording that 'the Association does not adopt a position if this is contrary to the vital and duly justified interests of one of its members' (*ibid.*). At this time, apart from this premise for vital and duly justified interests, a proposal could be adopted if three or more countries voted against it. Whilst there are constitutional possibilities for members to dissent through footnotes on policy positions, like voting, this is rarely used and is extremely cumbersome in that it is a constitutional requirement for this position to be mentioned every time the association's view is put forward.

---

[4] Article 19, Rules of Procedure.
[5] Article 7.1, Statutes.

Nonetheless, the organisation is not paralysed by its formal procedures, and it is not possible for a small band of peripheral members to hold the organisation to ransom. When George Jacobs took up his term of office as President[6] in 1998, he signalled his intention to change the structure of the consensus system. He told the *Financial Times* that:

> The consensus approach has worked well for us on most issues, but it has its limits. My aim is to come up with a system that respects consensus as much as possible, but I do not want to say no on an issue when a large majority is in favour. (Smith, 1998: 10)

The result was the QMV system of majority voting agreed in late 1999, described above. In practice, despite an equality of weight in voting between countries,[7] there is an informal understanding that extra efforts are made to accommodate the largest members, particularly on matters of some importance to them, and when the largest members[8] speak there is an extra resonance. There is also a weighting towards the EU members, in that the Rules of Procedure that 'the members from EU countries may decide to issue a position paper on a Community matter on their own collective behalf. In this case, the non EU members play a consultative role' (*ibid.*: 4).[9]

The Secretary General of UNICE also has an influence, and a key one, over the speed of decision-making, in filtering draft policy positions emerging from the five policy committees[10] from the Executive Committee. Policy Committees meet approximately three times a year, and this greatly regulates the speed of decision-taking within UNICE. Those that do not establish a new position, or significantly deviate from previously approved policy, can be issued by the approval of the Secretary General, without further deliberation by the Executive Committee. As well as the criteria of speed, this scrutiny provides for an essential coordinating role in ensuring that position papers coming from the policy committees, discussed below, are mutually consistent. Prudence in exercising this function on the part of the Secretary General is bound to lean on the side of risk-aversion and the consequent lengthening of decision-making times.

---

[6] The President of UNICE is empowered to choose his or her own Vice-Presidents for 18-month periods, and to use these as a sounding board and advice group in the shape of the Group of Vice-Presidents, and an aid to decision-making. The model of a 'group of presidents' is frequently used in other EU business associations.

[7] A country vote is divided between members where there is more than one affiliate from that country. A member from the state concerned has the right to veto a new membership application from an association in that country.

[8] See note 1. Note that the four largest members pay almost twice as much as the next largest.

[9] Article 12, Rules of Procedure.

[10] The five policy committees are: Economic and Financial Affairs; Company Affairs; Industrial Affairs; External Relations; Social Affairs.

Representative organisations with an active constituency require mechanisms that encourage the participation of their members (a function of the 'logic of membership'). To be credible with the institutions they engage, they also need to demonstrate sound competence in the technical areas covered (a function of the 'logic of influence'). The usual mechanism to achieve this is the establishment of technical working groups whose draft positions are filtered through further, political, tiers of authority. In this, UNICE is no different to most other business associations, in that each of the five policy committees of UNICE are empowered to establish specialist working groups. There are currently some 60 working groups operating under the authority of these policy committees, each producing draft policy positions, raising the need for coordination discussed above. Sometimes, working groups generate their own sub-groups, which in turn can extend time horizons and complexities in reaching policy positions. However, because committees have a tendency to outlive the functions for which they are established, and entrepreneurs associated with them start to generate solutions in search of problems, working groups are constitutionally required to be provided with a specific working remit to be accomplished within a specified period of time. The discipline of deadlines is therefore designed to assist the process of reaching decisions in a timely manner. Any working groups that are not '*ad hoc*' require Executive Committee approval at the outset.

Membership of UNICE working groups can be much sought after by organisations seeking the authority and endorsement of the association, or by those in pursuit of other agendas, including 'spoilers' wishing to prevent UNICE from taking up a damaging position for them. The association tends to respond positively to requests for membership of these groups from those claiming special knowledge, whether from other EU business associations, companies, or other organisations. Where individuals are in a position to offer support, ways and means are found to include them as part of the working group, provided that the group does not grow too large and is not captured by any one particular type of contested interest. Requests from companies offering support are processed through seeking a nomination from a national member association of UNICE. Formally, EU business associations can attend working group meetings as observers, though in practice they carry as much weight as other members. There have been instances where individuals from an EU business association have been appointed to the Chair of a sub-group. In this way, active and organised EU business associations can achieve much, and those such as CEFIC and EFPIA have advanced their own agendas considerably. This possibility was specifically investigated in the research design, with a '3' weighting factor (Chapter 3). Twelve of the 14 organisations that could be rated on this criteria achieving a score of '4' or '5', of whom one-half were in the top quartile of associations. There have also been instances where the perspectives of sectoral associations have caused conflict in an organisation representing business-wide views, and on a small number of occasions a member of the secretariat has needed to insist that only the views of the national members can be taken. Nonetheless, the value that is attached to the badge of an official UNICE position, and the efforts undertaken to obtain it, provides some clue to the status of the organisation within the Brussels public affairs community.

The profile of UNICE as a whole in the survey is one that might be expected of a representative, business-wide association with high profile, active national members. It scored highly ('4') on the benefits of membership, including its use by members for lobbying, though higher still ('5') on the 'costs of non-member-ship', in that exit could not really be an option for a serious national business-wide association seeking to protect its members' interests through participation. Thus, the association achieved a '5' rating on 'threat of exit' and the 'extent of evaluation undertaken'. Linked to these factors is the factor 'collective cloak', particularly as UNICE assumes the function of an employers' association, or sometimes may need to take up positions on behalf of its members that might be unpopular in public perception, such as seeking limits on environmental or con-sumer protection. Hence, the 'collective cloak' factor also attracted a '5' rating. The extent of UNICE activities in external trade representation, including those with the World Trade Organisation (WTO), also make this a '5'-rated factor, pro-viding coherence within UNICE with a mission to input a 'European' business perspective. This 'European' mission leads to a score of '4' to reflect the extent to which its members are involved in European-wide markets.

Again as might be expected, ratings below '3' were obtained on the factors 'member activity in Brussels', and the related factor 'counter-lobbying by mem-bers'. This, together with the high weighting of the 'cost of non-membership' fac-tor, helps to explain the low degree of autonomy from its members. Its breadth explains the low rating on the factor 'degree of firms of similar size', and, as extensively discussed above, its proneness to lowest-common-denominator posi-tions. There is a high degree of reassurance provided by the consistency in the linkage between these factors, and from what might be expected of an organisa-tion with the profile of UNICE. Perhaps more difficult to predict at the outside is the EU Committee of the American Chamber of Commerce (AMCHAM- EU), in that it has a much more selective constituency. As such, where prediction is possi-ble, what might be expected from this is the 'mirror image' of advantages and disadvantages.

AMCHAM-EU: 'THE EU COMMITTEE'

The EU Committee of the American Chamber of Commerce describes itself as 'the voice of American business in Europe' (www.eucommittee.be). Originating from a panel of the American Chamber of Commerce in Belgium in the 1960s, it obtained a separate budget and membership status in the 1980s. It currently represents 135 firms of American parentage. This level of membership is only marginally reduced from a previous peak of 142 following a recent 10 per cent hike in membership fees. These 142 members are listed in Table 5.2.

Table 5.2   Members of the EU Committee of the American Chamber of Commerce

Abbott Laboratories	Adamson BSMG	Agilent Technologies	A.I.G.	Akin, Gump, Strauss, Hauer & Feld	Alcoa Europe
American Express	AOL Europe	AOL Time Warner	Amway	Arthur Andersen	Ashurst Morris Crisp
AT&T	Avon Products	Baker & McKenzie	Baxter World Trade	Becton Dickinson	Bellsouth
Black and Decker	Boeing International	Bristol-Myers Squibb	British American Tobacco	Cargill	Caterpillar
Chiquita	Chiron	Chubb Insurance Company	Citibank	Cleary, Gotlieb, Steen & Hamilton	Clifford Chance Pünder
Coca-Cola	Compaq	Concert	Corning	Coudert Brothers, Coppens Van Ommesleghe & Faures	Covington & Burling
Daimler Chrysler	Dechert Price & Rhoads	Dell	DHL Worldwide Network	Dorsey & Whitney LLP	Dow Corning
Dow Europe	Dun & Bradstreet	Du Pont de Nemours	Eamonn Bates Europe	Edelman	EDS
Eli Lilly	Emerson Electric Co.	EPPA	Ernst & Young	ExxonMobil Chemical	ExxonMobil
Federal Express	Foley & Lardner	Ford	Freshfields Bruckhaus Deringer	General Electric	General Motors
Gillette	Glaxo SmithKline	Goldman Sachs	GPC	Grayling Political Strategy	Guardian Europe
Hercules	Hewlett Packard	Hill & Knowlton	Hogan & Hartson	Honeywell	Hunton & Williams
IBM	Instinet	Intel	Intergraph	International Paper	Johnson & Johnson

Table 5.2   Continued

Jones, Day, Reavis & Pogue	Keller & Heckman	Kellogg's	Kimberly-Clark	Kodak	KPMG
Kraft Foods	Le Boeuf, Lamb, Green & MacRae	Levi Strauss	Linklaters & Alliance	Lovells	Lucent Technologies
3M	Mars	Mastercard	Mattel	McDonald's	McKinsey & Co.
Merck Sharp & Dohme	Merial	Microsoft	Monsanto	Morgan, Lewis & Bockius	Morgan Stanley
Morrison & Foerster	Motorola	Nalco	NCR	Nike	Nortel Networks
Oppenheimer, Wolff & Donnelly	ORACLE	Pennzoil	Pfizer	Philip Morris	Pioneer
Price Waterhouse Coopers	Procter & Gamble	Qualcomm	Reebok	Reliant Energy	Rohm & Haas
SBC Communications	Skadden, Arps, Slate, Meagher & Flom	Solutia	Squire, Sanders & Dempsey	StorageTek	Sun Microsystems
Texaco	United Parcel Service	United Technologies Corporation	Van Bael & Bellis	Verizon Communications	Viacom
VNU World Directories	Vodafone Group Services Ltd	Walt Disney Company	Weber Shandwick	Weil, Gotshal & Manges LLP	Western Union
White & Case LLP	Wilmer, Cutler & Pickering	W L Gore & Associates	Worldcom		

Source: http://www.eucommittee.be/Pages/fsprof9.htm

Despite this increase in affiliation fees, the organisation remains relatively cheap to affiliate to at a fee level a shade under €9000, which is a fraction of the cost of affiliating to many of the other large EU business associations. Cost forms no part of the membership calculation of its members. These are primarily drawn from large American companies already with a public affairs presence in Brussels, for whom membership of the EU Committee is mostly seen as essential. For this constituency, joining the EU Committee appears to be seen as 'the thing to do', on the basis of the quality of the network which comprises the organisations, the information available, and the many opportunities to participate in its work and draw from its reputation. It is not therefore really suitable for firms without public affairs personnel already in Brussels, which helps explain non-membership of eligible organisations such as Union Carbide (with a public affairs function based in Switzerland) and Hercules Europe (with a Belgian public affairs function located some distance from Brussels). There are, however, some exceptions of large US firms with a public affairs function in Brussels and who are not members of the EU Committee, such as those in the IT and airlines sectors. This phenomenon is currently a topic of further research underway with the author.

These exceptions apart, 'the thing to do' explanation of membership behaviour, as well as being informed by networking purposes, is also informed by a sense of membership identity. This identity originates from the common American heritage and the common size. The EU Committee primarily organises large multinationals of US parentage which share a common outlook in liberal, open markets. This common identity, based on the dual facets of commonality of size and national origin, greatly enhances associational coherence. The national origin basis of this has found a variety of outlets over time. In the mid-1990s it found expression through concerns among US firms that European standardisation structures, such as CEN, had been used by European firms as a means of erecting closet technical barriers to the entry of non-European products into the European economic area. This 'common enemy' factor has historically extended to the exclusion of US firms from European business associations, although the structure of global business has now led to the inclusion of these in domestic business associations, and consequently in EU business associations. Few EU business associations that admit companies directly now discriminate in member admission policies between European and US business. The EU Committee, on the other hand, continues to benefit from its own US focus, with membership rules designed to protect its American identity, such as constitutional limits on the number of affiliations from non-US firms (see, for instance, Table 5.2 where a small number of European firms are included). This US identity is strengthened by the presence of the European– American Industrial Council, operating from the same building as the EU Committee and closely linked to it. This organisation is modelled on the European Round Table of Industrialists (Cowles, 1996), comprising a group of chief executive officers responsible for the European operations of US multinationals. Whilst it has been a much lower-key organisation, it does provide a forum for business leaders of EU Committee members at the highest level to engage EU politicians at the highest level. Thus, it has regularly drawn in speakers to its events of the calibre of the President of the Commission. It contributes to the overall concept of identity with and governability of the EU Committee; and it helps the EU Committee address what it lacks by way of natural institutional ties that UNICE, by virtue of its status as the broad representative of European business, enjoys.

EU Committee members include 40 of the top Fortune 100 major American companies. In addition to its full members, its category of associate membership (for firms providing services to its membership constituency) attracts firms to the extent that it is frequently oversubscribed and has a waiting list. In addition to its membership constituency through affiliation, the EU Committee coordinates EU Affairs for the European Council of American Chambers of Commerce, which has 16 000 member companies representing over $225 billion of US investment in Europe. These factors are bound to make it an authoritative voice on the Brussels scene.

The qualitative insights from interviews indicate that the EU Committee is seen by companies as a forum to meet people and to strengthen an individual lobbying position through acquiring the strong name of the organisation behind it. As a result of this pull, the organisation has historically helped socialise American member companies in the ways of Brussels public affairs, and in particular the more 'softly, softly' diplomacy required of them in contrast to the more brash and aggressive styles of Washington (Gardner, 1991), although traces of this latter style are still evident in some documents from these sources. Today, however, the practice of many US firms in hiring Europeans to undertake their EU public affairs means that member socialisation has become a less important role of the EU Committee. The EU Committee is not, however, afraid to speak its mind, and sees engagement of public opinion as part of its role more than some other business-wide associations (Cowles, 1996). This 'collective cloak' factor adds value for its membership.

As described in Chapter 1, the EU Committee is a membership-driven organisation, drawing upon 650 individuals from its 12 specialist sub-committees and (currently, 38) *ad hoc* working groups. This culture of a membership-driven organisation explains a relatively low level of staffing, in that members take forward much of the work of the organisation, assisted by the secretariat. Thus, whilst the employment of 20 or so staff appears a relatively high figure in comparison to other EU business associations, it is small for the range of functions that it undertakes. In drawing heavily upon the Brussels public affairs offices of its members, it has frequently been able to speak, literally, with a European accent, in that many of these personnel are European in origin. This has helped with its identity in Brussels, but also with building coherence in that members from similarly sized companies frequently meet up in a relatively confined setting which helps foster trust, which in turn helps build coherence to the work of an association (Chapter 3). These ties, and the experience of working together in the EU Committee, have been a common force for change in other EU associations (Cowles, 1996).

Apart from the quality of its network, the EU Committee has a strong reputation for the high quality and authoritative nature of its publications and reports, and its ability to draw from the business practices of its members in guiding the work of the organisation. Hence, its regular strategic reviews are robust and adept in setting priorities, guided by the principle of always seeking to position itself as part of the solution rather than part of the problem. In general, it is successful in this mission, in that it is regarded within the Commission as a supportive ally in favour of European integration. Its review process also helps it to address the weaknesses identified by its members. Lists of the latter, drawn from the author's interviews with members and from the organisation's own literature, have included: an overproduction of information (processing 90 000 documents per month on average); its relations with the Parliament and with the member states; and the extent of coordination between sub-committees and in consequence the consistencies of its positions (EU Committee, 2001). Nonetheless, its ability to incorporate business practices ensure that it is among the more adaptable associations in Brussels to changes in circumstance, while it is also among the quickest to arrive at common positions. The disadvantage of an 'outsider' tag is counterbalanced by the stimulus this provides to member unity, and the present EU Affairs Manager sees the absence of ties to any particular member state interest as a potential positional strength in public affairs.

These factors are reflected in the analysis of the EU Committee undertaken in the survey. It scores highly on factors such as a collective cloak, its orientation to open rather than national markets, the degree of firms of similar size, member trust, and the basis of membership for both benefits and the cost of non-membership. The nature of the organisation, based around member offices in Brussels, means that it attracted a low score for the degree of member activity in Brussels, although this is not a significant issue in that the organisation also scored highly on the degree of member discipline behind its common positions. It remains a highly coherent, high-reputation association on the Brussels scene, largely on the basis of its common identity in representing large American firms.

THE ERT

The European Round Table of Industrialists (ERT) is a forum of (currently, 46) European industrial leaders (at chief executive officer (CEO), or Chairman, level), which records its aim as 'to strengthen Europe's economy and improve its global competitiveness' (www.ert.be). It is not a lobby organisation, but a strategy and visionary outfit aimed at inserting 'big issues' into the EU policy agenda. Membership of the organisation is personal rather than corporate, and by invitation only (Table 5.3). These invitations are only extended to the leaders of large

Table 5.3   Members of the European Round Table of Industrialists

Name of member	Company
Morris Tabaksblat (Chairman)	Reed Elsevier
Gerhard Cromme (Vice-Chairman)	ThyssenKrupp
Carlo De Benedetti (Vice-Chairman)	Cofide-Cir
Américo Amorim	Amorim
Percy Barnevik	Investor
Jean-Louis Beffa	Saint-Gobain
Peter Bonfield	BT
Peter Brabeck-Letmathe	Nestlé
Antony Burgmans	Unilever
Roberto Colaninno	Olivetti
Alfonso Cortina	Repsol YPD
Bertrand Collomb	Lafarge
Thierry Desmarest	TotalFinaElf
Dimitris Daskalopoulos	Delta Holding
Jean-René Fourtou	Aventis
Paolo Fresco	Fiat
José Antonio Garrido	Iberdrola
Jukka Härmälä	Stora Enso Oyj
Ulrich Hartmann	E.ON
Franz Humer	F. Hoffmann-La Roche
Daniel Janssen	Solvay
Alain Joly	Air Liquide
Jak Kamhi	Profilo Holding
Gerard Kleisterlee	Royal Philips Electronics
Cees van Lede	Akzo Nobel
David Lees	GKN
André Leysen	Gevaert
Flemming Lindeløv	Carlsberg
Gérard Mestrallet	Suez Lyonnaise des Eaux
Charles Miller Smith	ICI
Egil Myklebust	Norsk Hydro
Jorma Ollila	Nokia
Heinrich von Pierer	Siemens
Hasso Plattner	SAP
Lars Ramqvist	Ericsson
Paolo Scaroni	Pilkington
Richard Schenz	OMV
Manfred Schneider	Bayer
Louis Schweitzer	Renault
George Simpson	Marconi
Michael Smurfit	Jefferson Smurfit
Ron Sommer	Deutsche Telekom
Peter Sutherland	BP
Marco Tronchetti Provera	Pirelli
Phil Watts	Royal Dutch/Shell
Jürgen Weber	Deutsche Lufthansa

Source: ERT (2001b); http://www.ert.be/pc/enc_frame.htm

and important European firms, with around half of ERT members included among the largest 100 transnational corporations in the world (van Apeldoorn, 2001). The organisation claims that the combined turnover of its members is over €850 billion, and employ over four million people worldwide (ERT, 2001a). These are listed in Table 5.3.

A recent *Financial Times* article marvelled at the reputation of the ERT in achieving its aim, in comparison to its relatively humble offices and small secretariat (Betts, 2001). The article recites a familiar story of how policy-makers, analysts and critics alike have credited the organisation with agenda-setting many of the big ideas which have come to dominate the EU agenda. The most well-known of these stories concerns the role of the organisation in agenda-setting and helping the European Commission to achieve the shared goal of a European single market project. This story, first popularised by Cowles, has been extensively used to provide evidence of how the relationship between the European Commission and outside interests can be used to explain the course of European integration (see, for instance, Cowles, 1995).

In support of this account of the role of the ERT in the single market project, the *FT* article cites Jacques Delors in recalling that 'The ERT was the right vehicle. Unice could not have done it. Discussions with the ERT were simple and straightforward' (*ibid.*: 16). The clout of the ERT, with its CEO involvement from household-name firms, undoubtedly made this 'the right vehicle' through which to build the support necessary among member states. Certainly, the relationship between Delors, on the look out for supportive allies, and the ERT was a close one, with the two partners appearing together at press conferences. Cowles recounts how ERT members worked alongside, cajoled and even threatened member state governments to achieve the necessary political support (Cowles, 1995).

According to some sources, this influence has prevailed. The *FT* article cites a recent description of the ERT by the UK *Guardian* national newspaper as 'a shadowy lobby group that has, for the past 15 years, exerted an iron grip on policy making in Brussels' (Betts, *op. cit.*). Similarly, a report entitled 'Misshaping Europe', claiming that 'the political agenda of the EU has to a large extent been dominated by the ERT', is also quoted by the *FT* article. Evidence provided for these claims included the role of the ERT in agenda-setting Trans-European Networks (TENs), the benchmarking of EU policies, and most recently in the development of a ten-year EU economic and social strategy agreed under the 2000 Portuguese presidency (Betts, *op. cit.*). The ERT's own literature also presents its achievements in setting the climate of ideas from which public policy events have arisen (ERT, 2001c). Among these are listed: work on lifelong learning and investing in knowledge; information highways; climate change; competitiveness; and 'pressure to help close the Uruguay Round negotiations' in world trade negotiations (www.ert.be). These perceptions appear to have provided much of the inspiration for the creation of an opposing pressure group, Corporate Europe Observatory, whose exposé-style literature also contributes to the 'ERT rules OK' model (see Balanyá *et al.*, 2000).

Certainly, evidence taken from friend, foe and propaganda alike provide a powerful case for the strength of the ERT. Its consistent role as an ally of the Commission in promoting European integration is reflected in the preamble to its objectives, stating that 'Europeans can only solve their problems by closer co-operation' (www.ert.be). Undoubtedly, the Commission and the ERT have been mutual influences; but it is also easy to exaggerate the case. The ERT participates in the rarefied atmosphere of 'high politics', in which its voice is just one of a number seeking influence upon public policies, alongside forces such as national governments and the international environment. Undoubtedly it contributes to the climate of debate and to the influences upon some of these decision-making forces; but the simple connection should not be made between its demands and public policy outcomes, nor should its creation be seen as a response to the evident weaknesses of UNICE in the early 1980s. Its history is better understood as an astute initiative led by the CEOs of large firms in the EFTA countries, concerned about a 'Fortress Europe' and, excluded from large-firm EC organisation, seeking to gain an inside track in the EC. Later, as it developed into an organisation with mainstream EC membership credentials under different leadership, it too could sometimes look like a protectionist lobby seeking to persuade the Commission to restrict Japanese imports, particularly cars and electronics. One perspective is that it obtained these favours in return for providing support for some other of the policy initiatives of Jacques Delors, such as those in social policy fields. This perspective motivated free traders, in turn, to seek entry into the organisation. Undoubtedly it has made its presence felt, although it is an open question whether it remains as influential today as at the peak of the Delors days. Some members in recent years have chosen to leave the ERT, while others have allowed their membership to lapse through a lack of participation.

The strength of the ERT undoubtedly derives from its membership profile and format. Its policy positions are built directly by its members, with one CEO being asked to take the lead on a particular issue through a working party. This member company will then use its informal networks with others in order to build a position before returning to the formal structures of the ERT, consisting of a steering committee of seven members followed by presentation in one of the twice-yearly plenary meetings. In addition to written communiqués and publications in which its positions are presented, members are used to drive the message forward at the highest level through face-to-face communication with Europe's leading politicians and policy-makers (van Apeldoorn, 2001). This lean, flexible membership-driven structure, together with its cohesiveness and ability to come to rich common positions, is much admired elsewhere. Whilst many of these plaudits are deserved, it does enjoy a number of natural advantages. Its membership constituency is highly selective and relatively homogenous in both the size and structure of firms, and in drawing upon CEOs with broadly similar world-views. As Bastian van Apeldoorn (2000) comments, it has no members to either represent or to discipline, and does not face 'governability problems'. CEOs are in a unique position to lend the name of their company to ERT positions, and they are not challenged by the same issues of public affairs coordination as confronts company public affairs managers in trying to establish and reconcile the interests of different divisions of a firm, from a much less powerful position.

Another natural advantage of the ERT when compared to other organisations is that it is highly selective in the issues it chooses to develop. It is a unique organisation, and as a strategic think-tank in purpose, drawing upon CEOs for its membership, it is not easy to draw lessons from which operational business interest organisations can benefit. Nonetheless, it is worth noting that it has been the source for a small number of other groups, such as the Association for the Monetary Union of Europe (AMUE), the European Centre for Infrastructure Studies (ECIS) (to take up the work on Trans European Networks, TENs), and the European Roundtable of Financial Services. The ideas of seeking the involvement of CEOs, and a flat structure of decision-making, have been the sources of inspiration for change among other EU associations. This means that it is now somewhat less unique among EU public affairs organisations, and to a certain extent its energy has been absorbed by its institutionalisation into the EU political system (van Apeldoorn, 2001). It is now somewhat different as an organisation from the one created in the early 1980s, and credited with the impetus for the creation of the single market. Then, it began as an astute initiative by the EFTA companies to gain an inside track in the EC in response to a perception that the EC was in danger of turning into a 'Fortress Europe'. Later, under different leadership, it is perceived by some as adopting a more protectionist lobby against Japanese imports, particularly in the IT and automobile domains, and there are business insiders who link its historic influence to its willingness to support the Delors social agenda. In response to this perception, it attracted a much wider base of membership from transnational companies anxious to use the organisation to promote a free trade agenda, and it is this sense of identity that contributes greatly to the sense of coherence of the modern ERT.

The somewhat unique nature of the ERT makes it very difficult to apply the research design developed for traditional EU business associations, although a number of the points above are reflected in the scores attributed. Thus, the common ideology of open European markets is reflected in a score of '5' for 'European or national markets', and the foundation of large firms provides for a score of '5' on the factor 'degree of firms of similar size'. Similarly, the exclusive nature of the organisation finds expression in the '5' scores for the factors 'issue-niche organisation' and 'membership for benefits of membership'. High scores were also recorded for the factors 'trust between members' (because of the 'bosses club' profile of the organisation based around a limited number of individuals), its ability to come to common positions with a relatively high degree of coherence, and the degree of EU identity in global trade presented by the organisation. Whilst the ERT is not itself a participant in the Transatlantic Business Dialogue (TABD), many of its members are central figures on the European side of the table, and provide the ERT with important transatlantic links. The exclusivity of the organisation, its foundation around business leaders drawn from European firms, its focus at the strategic level and the common ideology of members make this a very highly governable organisation.

EUROCHAMBRES

On the front page of its website, EUROCHAMBRES (Association of European Chambers of Commerce) announces itself as 'the voice of business' and 'the largest European business representation' with 34 national chamber organisations as full members, and 1300 chambers of commerce and industry, together representing 14 million enterprises. Claiming that 95 per cent of these are SMEs, other pages announce itself as 'the acknowledged spokesman of SMEs at the European institutions in Brussels' (www.eurochambres.be). There are few associated with the organisation that would take these descriptions at face value, and still fewer outside it. Since its formation in 1958, EUROCHAMBRES has struggled to live up to these claims and has fought, unsuccessfully, to be treated with parity by the EU institutions alongside UNICE, and even UEAPME. Its strongest institutional ties are with the Committee of the Regions, where its network of regional chambers finds a valued partner. This dependence upon an institution with consultative powers only in the European policy process is itself an indicator of centrality of the organisation.

Of all the cross-constituency organisations reviewed in this section, EUROCHAMBRES has the greatest difficulty in reaching common positions and the most apparent weaknesses of coherence. Some of its members describe it more as a large network than a business interest association. The network is one of its principal strengths, covering most of the landmass of Europe (together with embracing Russia and Israel). This profile enables it to undertake significant development work with business organisations in Central and Eastern Europe, and in doing so assists with the construction of democratic mechanisms in the region in supporting fledgling business interest representatives. The network finds value in projects such as agreement with the Commission to locate many European Information Centres within the premises of regional chambers of commerce, or contractor to the Commission for studies on issues such as training in quality for SMEs (EUROCHAMBRES, 1998). These are familiar examples of the ways in which the European Commission supports and nurtures the development of EU-level interest organisations in the hope of creating mechanisms of European integration, first identified by neo-functionalist accounts. But these types of functions can also be a source of weakness, in that it diverts the organisation from its work in political representation. A whole department is devoted to Chamber Network Development, while another helps chambers in the application of new information and communication technologies. One half of the 18 staff of EUROCHAMBRES work on developing the capacities of its network members (including training and development), pooling the expertise of its network (e.g. export promotions), and matchmaking SMEs with commercial partners elsewhere through its links with other global chambers of commerce, including those in the US, Japan and Latin America. The strength of its global network is also emphasised through its formal co-operation agreements with chambers of commerce in China and Korea. These global links, its function as a network and its service orientation, are its principal strengths as an association. Of all the business-wide associations reviewed in this chapter, it is the most service-oriented organisation, and the least well-suited for political representation at the EU level.

Its members are quite different in their needs, strength, structure and demands. This diversity largely results from their different status, with some (eight members) recognised in public law based on compulsory membership, with others based on voluntary membership and establishment in private law. Some national members are themselves extremely weak, such as Portugal with 1800 members and Ireland with 8000, while others are strong, such as Italy with well over 4 million, and the Wirtschaftskammer Österreich (WKO), the largest Austrian business-wide association. National chambers from Italy, Austria, Germany, the UK, France, Spain, the Netherlands and Luxembourg operate as an informal Executive Committee overseeing the work of the secretariat (Institut des Sciences du Travail, 1999). However, the WKÖ is the only EUROCHAMBRES member to participate in collective bargaining at the national level, and enjoys a mandate from its members to do so. For this reason, EUROCHAMBRES does not wish to participate in the negotiation of agreements likely to lead to binding directives under social partnership arrangements, although it does wish to take part in the consultation phases of social dialogue at the invitation of the European Commission. It is thus a 'second level' social partner, and is recognised for this purpose in the definitive documentation of the Commission.[11]

---

[11] COM (98) 322 final of 20 May 1998.

This diversity is also present in the expectations that members have of the organisation. Members from Central and Eastern Europe (CEE) tend to look to EUROCHAMBRES to provide them with credibility in their own countries as they seek to establish their own identities and independence from state structures. Small members, and those members from countries that are weakly represented elsewhere in EU business representational structures, look to the organisation for political representation, whereas those with alternatives do not. Because the organisation sees itself as a loose collection of independent members, it has little difficulty with its members undertaking their own political representation activities in the EU. Eleven of the 34 national chamber organisations have their own Brussels offices, of which just one, the smallest, is located within the same building as EUROCHAMBRES. A number of the large city chambers, including Milan, Madrid and Frankfurt, have their own separate network organisation outside of EUROCHAMBRES.

The formal voting structures of EUROCHAMBRES appear geared towards substantive majority positions, rather than consensus, although the reality is more directed at consensus than might be evident from a formal reading of the rules. The supreme decision-making body is the Plenary Assembly, meeting twice each year in Brussels, where decisions are taken with a two-thirds majority based on the weighted votes of members. However, where a unanimous decision is not obtained, the position of those dissenting is attached to the majority position, meaning that in practice the ability of a single member to post a different view alongside the main one turns the balance towards consensus seeking in the hope of single position. This leads to heavily compromised positions, with substantial powers vested in any one single member. The Executive Committee, or Conseil d'Administration, includes at least six delegates voted for a year each, renewable for an unlimited number of times, and is empowered to pass resolutions which define the general policy of EUROCHAMBRES as well as overseeing day-to-day management.

A number of EUROCHAMBRES members are openly critical of the organisation and its top-heavy structures of making policy, though of interest is that a member never leaves. Even when the UK national chamber of commerce organisation recently conducted consultations among its own affiliates about remaining in membership, it found that they wished it to remain part of the EUROCHAMBRES network, emphasising some degree of perceived value. At least, for affiliates of national members, there are very few cost implications of remaining in membership, whereas the alternatives might imply higher costs to be borne by them in the establishment of independent channels of representation. In any event, there are no alternative EU associations organising chambers of commerce, and EUROCHAMBRES does provide a network which most national chambers feel they need at the EU level. Affiliates of national chambers also benefit directly from the business services provided by EUROCHAMBRES, such as training and export advice, as well as from the collaborative projects that EUROCHAMBRES has undertaken with the Commission, such as the impact of VAT on firms, transport policy and regional development (Claveloux, 1993). Members also appreciate the geographical extent of the network, including member associations from outside Europe, and the opportunities these provide as a means of promoting international trade issues. Most EUROCHAMBRES members accept the organisation for what it is, and have relatively low expectations of it as a political player. At least until a recent change of leadership, this view was also strongly present among the secretariat. In this climate, the organisation might best be evaluated in its own terms rather than against criteria of governability.

Given these considerations, the appearance of EUROCHAMBRES in penultimate place in Table 4.3 should come as little surprise to the reader. Its average score was 2.1, it did not attract a rating on any factor above '3,' and was rated the lowest '1' on a number of criteria of governability. These included the degree of member activity in Brussels, the low dependence by members upon it for lobbying, its proneness to lowest-common-denominator positions, and the low expectation by members for membership benefits. Once again, it is worth making the wider comment that this analysis should not be interpreted as criticism of EUROCHAMBRES; rather, it simply reflects the reality that this association has structural properties that lead to very low governability. Its members are highly diverse in their significance in the national setting, and their composition. For affiliates of national chambers of commerce there are many alternative avenues for those seeking political representation at the EU level, ranging from national business associations that are members of UNICE, to the regional representations in Brussels. There are now approaching 170 of these, and the best resourced, drawn from the German Länder and the Spanish communidades autónomas, employ more staff than does EUROCHAMBRES. EUROCHAMBRES members do not therefore look to the organisation for political representation at the highest level in Brussels. Under these circumstances, a low degree of governability is somewhat unsurprising.

UEAPME

The European Association of Craft, Small and Medium-Sized Enterprises (UEAPME) is the leading representative of small and medium-sized enterprises (SMEs) in Europe. Its 26 full national association members from the 15 EU member states claim a membership of 7 million enterprises in Europe, with 30 million employees. These figures provide an indication of the rather fragmented constituency profile from which UEAPME draws. Among the notable points of its profile:

- It contains members such as the Wirtschaftskammer Österreich (WKO), the largest Austrian business-wide association whose home is UEAPME because it is excluded from UNICE (see note 1).
- Six UEAPME members are also members of UNICE, either directly or by affiliation (Institute des Sciences du Travail, 1999).
- Five UEAPME members, from Germany, France and Spain, have affiliations in excess of 800 000 members (*ibid.*). One Italian member, Confartigianato, has 420 000 members. These members, together with the WKÖ, provide the most significant backbone of UEAPME.
- Nine of its members have a formal role in cross-industry collective bargaining, and 11 organisations participate in formalised consultation with cross-industry tripartite bodies (*ibid.*)
- The principal representative organisations of SMEs in some member states, most significantly the UK, are not in membership.
- Five UEAPME members have less than 5000 SME affiliates (Institute des Sciences du Travail, 1999). There is a problem of lack of participation among some UEAPME members.
- SME populations differ greatly across member states, and representation tends to be highly fragmented within member states.
- There is a very significant population of SMEs in German-speaking Europe, and consequently many of the EU-level SME organisations have a strong German flavour to them, whether in location, personnel, membership or some combination of these. UEAPME shares some of these tendencies, with a location in Bonn until 1990, the background of its German General Secretary as a member of the German Parliament for almost 20 years, and its most powerful affiliate being a German member.

The fragmented and variable organisation of SME interests at the national level is reflected in EU organisation. UEAPME is itself the product of an amalgamation of various EU SME organisations, dating from 1979, and recently underwent a significant merger with the next largest EU SME organisation, EUROPMI (European Committee for Small and Medium-Sized Independent Companies) in 1999. At stages during the past decade there have been up to 15 EU-level organisations claiming to be a cross-sectoral SME representative association, and recognised in some way by the (then) DG XXIII (Müller, 1997). Whilst there has been some consolidation of these in recent years, there has also been further diversification. Thus, the recent merger between UEAPME and EUROPMI took place against the backdrop of the creation of the European

Small Business Alliance (ESBA) in the same year. ESBA includes the largest small-business organisation in the UK, the Federation of Small Businesses, which shoulders much of the administrative responsibilities, though it only has significant other small-business organisations in Germany, France, Sweden and Austria, and a presence in Brussels through a consultancy. Another organisation still, based on a different model, is 'Growth Plus', founded in 1995 as 'Europe's 500' with co-funding from (then) DG XXIII. This is a club of the fastest growing firms in Europe (in 1999, around 120 paying members), whose brand appeal has been commercially developed by the association management company which runs the organisation. Still another organisation relatively recent to the SME scene in Brussels (1994) with a somewhat unusual profile is CEA-PME (European Confederation of Associations of Small and Medium-Sized Enterprises), whose German-dominated membership includes taxpayers' associations. There are some superficial likenesses with UEAPME in that the organisation has a similar sounding name and acronym, origins in Bonn, Germany,[12] a larger than life German General Secretary as well as powerful Germanic members, and each share a common member. However, the likeness ends there in that CEA-PME has fewer pretensions as a political representative and tries to concentrate more on a selective range of services. Operating from cramped offices in Brussels and in part dependent upon internships, it is a somewhat hyperactive outfit organising activities such as public demonstrations on behalf of taxpayer interests on such issues as 'the misuse of the Common Agricultural Policy'. Unsurprisingly, its relationship with UEAPME is somewhat problematic.

Other EU small-business organisations include the European Confederation of Self-Employed (CEDI), the European Association of the Middle Classes (AECM), and the European Medium and Small Business Union (EMSU). A recent report on the representativeness of these organisations for the European Commission (Institut des Sciences du Travail, 1999) in respect of their ability to participate in social partnership arrangements raised some questions about each of these three organisations. Thus, the study found it 'difficult to establish whether the CEDI is a German organisation with a European Vocation, or a genuinely European organisation as such' (p. 8), AECM did not wish to be considered as a candidate for inclusion in the social partnership, while the study could not elicit a response of any kind from attempts to contact EMSU. In addition to all these representative organisations, EUROCHAMBRES and UNICE each have a substantial derivative SME constituency. Nonetheless, this brief survey indicates that UEAPME is by some distance the lead EU SME organisation, albeit not a monopoly.

---

[12] CEAPME also has a Bonn office, whereas UEAPME moved from Bonn in 1990.

Indeed, in spite of this landscape of fragmentation, UEAPME is a surprisingly cohesive organisation. Apart from its status as a lead organisation, this cohesion derives from eight principal sources:

- Many of its members are significant and established players in domestic politics, and have the sophistication and the resources to contribute and participate fully in an EU association. As discussed below, member resources are heavily used in SME associations, and UEAPME is no exception. As an example of the tasks it undertakes, in 1997 the organisation mailed 2281 texts and 171 circulars to its members, with each of the latter being translated into four working languages. In addition, most of its committee meetings required simultaneous translation (UEAPME, 1997). These straightforward, logistical tasks are highly resource-intensive, and can be beyond the fiscal membership dues that SME associations can pay.
- Apart from the special position of the WKÖ and its members, there is a common interest among their derivative members by virtue of their common identities as SMEs.
- UEAPME is consulted by UNICE before taking positions on behalf of employers in the negotiation of the social dialogue. UEAPME representatives play a full part in preparatory meetings of the employers' group, and in plenary meetings with the European Trade Union Confederation (ETUC) (Institut des Sciences du Travail, 1999). UEAPME achieved this position late in 1998 by negotiation with UNICE following initiation of a number of cases in the European Court of Justice/Court of First Instance first initiated in 1996. The common goal to find a place at the social dialogue top table was for some years a unifying factor in the organisation.
- SMEs themselves do not have the resources to set up shop in Brussels and challenge or bypass their associations, and few SME interests are significant in the work of sector associations, meaning that SMEs rely upon their cross-sectoral organisations to be a voice for them.
- The absence of large-firm members places practical limits upon the consultation UEAPME can reasonably undertake, and there is a lack of participation from some members. These factors leave the association with a significant degree of autonomy to define what the interests of SMEs are.
- The organisation has incorporated the resources of its membership to good effect. Whilst there is a central secretariat of around 20 staff, some of these are on secondment from members. Many members have a small office on the same corridor as the UEAPME secretariat, and there is a strong collective, almost family, identity whereby members actively contribute to the work of UEAPME. One member has something more than a small office, in that the largest member, the German Zentralverband des Deutschen Handwerks (ZdH),

has nine staff working from its Brussels premises. These offices tend to take up particular tasks of UEAPME; one example is the role of the UK office representative of the Forum for Private Business (FPB) being responsible for managing the development of a UEAPME web presence (UEAPME, 1997). While the price of the proximate offices is a certain loss of autonomy, the practical arrangement whereby some of the individuals are self-employed entrepreneurs selling their part-time services to UEAPME limits this loss. This also helps limit the extent of autonomous member activities with the EU institutions, though UEAPME members in any event tend to belong to UEAPME for the positive benefits it brings in terms of lobbying and information, rather than from a wish to be in a position to control it.

- UEAPME has proved adept at entrepreneurial activity, such as the creation of NORMAPME, and the Academie Avignon. NORMAPME is the official representative of craft/trades and SMEs in the European standardisation bodies, and has spawned a structure in itself, comprising a Technical Advisory Committee and a number of working groups. The Academie Avignon is an institutional framework for European co-operation in the field of research and transfer of knowledge in favour of SMEs (Müller, 2001).

- The eighth support for cohesion comes from the highly supportive environment for SMEs provided by the Commission. Once again, this returns us to the theme of 'institutionalism', and the impact of political institutions on the capacities of business interest associations. One of the author's interview respondents, a General Secretary of a sector association, noted how 'everyone goes moist eyed when the subject of SMEs comes up'. Without doubt, SMEs are pushing at an open door within the Commission, whose policy-making officials go out of their way to seek out the views of SME representative organisations on their own policy initiatives, or who frequently commission research to gauge the impact of such initiatives upon SMEs. Commission initiatives directed at SMEs are by now too numerous to mention, but the prominence of them to EU enterprise policy, as the 'acorns of today and oak trees of tomorrow', over the past decade is plain to see. These include major initiatives ranging from the Delors White Paper on *Growth, Competitiveness and Employment*, to the most recent forward strategies developed at the Lisbon summit in 2000. Other important initiatives have included an ongoing series of multi-annual programmes aimed at detailed operational support for SMEs.

However, despite the positive impact that this supportive environment has upon SME associations, the Commission's embrace of them all, and its need to be even-handed in its dealings with them, can also be a source of weakness for them. None of them are entrusted with the task of acting as official observatory (essentially, information provider for policy-relevant purposes) to the EU on small business, a function undertaken by a consultancy network in the Netherlands.

These seven factors help platform-building within UEAPME. Whilst it is usual for the organisation to be able to reach common positions (the organisation claims that none have taken more than six months), it is also not unusual for it to reach a view that it is unable to reach a common position on an issue. There is no voting system whatsoever in place to resolve differences. Where these emerge, it often uses a system of majority and minority opinions, reasoning that where it is not possible for the organisation to come to a common view, it is better for the organisation to demonstrate the difficulties in doing so, and where the main points of difference lie. This can be a somewhat deeper role than the scenario presented in the quote from David White in Chapter 3 (p. 77), in that it is intended to suggest to policy-makers that legislation on an issue may not be possible, and as such can be a clever game if the intention is to preserve the status quo. Nonetheless, General Secretaries of EU business associations as a whole are divided as to this high-risk strategy, with others reasoning that they do not wish to 'wash their dirty linen in public'.

There is nothing unusual in the UEAPME's formal structures, in that it is governed by an Executive Committee, a Presidency group, an Administrative Council and the General Assembly. On strategy, the real power lies with an informal committee of General Secretaries drawn from the members. As with most EU business associations, the real engine-room of platform-building is in the functional committees, together with the working parties they spawn. UEAPME has eight, covering legal affairs, economic and fiscal issues, vocational training, external relations, environment, research and new technologies, and cultural affairs. These comprise members appointed by the member associations, with each committee able to appoint *ad hoc* working groups. It is the secretariat, however, rather than the members, who get the ball rolling by writing the initial position papers. This top-down starting point is quite different from an organisation like ERT, or the EU Committee, where the position papers are wholly created by the members, and raises some interesting issues related to the debate about autonomy and leadership first raised in Chapter 3. There, it was argued that an association develops autonomy where it provides leadership by shaping the perceptions of its members as to what their interests actually might be over a range of given issues. Browne (1977) terms this 'farming members', where the secretariat gain supporters on issues in order to legitimise staff positions on them, and to avoid conflict within the organisation. More than conflict avoidance, this approach helps build coherence in associations. This top-down approach is possible in an organisation representing SMEs like UEAPME where there can be a problem of member participation and the secretariat has the freedom to move.

In the survey, UEAPME achieved a '5' rating on the governability factors such as the dependence by members upon it for lobbying and for information, their perception of high membership benefits, the trust between members fostered by member offices in the same corridor and from their common sense of purpose, and minimal threat of exit. '4' scores were obtained on the lack of evaluation of membership, the degree of autonomy from members, the 'common enemy' factor, the extent to which it provides members with a 'collective cloak', the similarity of derivative constituency (firm size), and its ability to build coherent common positions. It is the only association analysed in this chapter to appear in the upper quartile for both the 'simple average' and the 'weighted average' (Table 4.3). Using the governability criteria developed through this research it scores highly, although this should be read in light of the qualifications made at the start of this chapter about the applicability of these criteria to business-wide associations.

CONCLUSIONS

It is worth returning to this last consideration at the end of this chapter. How applicable are the criteria of governability developed for domain-based associations, to business-wide associations? In this chapter, they have taken a secondary role to other types of information used to assess these organisations, because around one-third of factors developed for sectoral/domain-specific associations cannot be applied to the contexts in which business-wide associations operate. However, most of the business-wide associations could be assessed sensibly on three-quarters of the factors. Beyond these, the additional factors of governability for EU cross-sectoral business associations (as compared to sectoral associations) seem to relate to the extent of associational capacities that emerge from their role as employer organisations. Some of these impact upon the existing factors of governability identified in sector associations. What does emerge is that a different form of weighting might be used, or that factors might be subdivided or cross-referenced in some way. For instance:

- *Member Activities in Brussels.* All of the business-wide associations assessed in this chapter are surrounded by member offices in Brussels to an extent not generally found among sector associations. As reviewed in this chapter, these offices can be a mixed blessing. Whilst they add to the resources of the EU association, enhance national channels of communication and develop intra member trust, they can also reduce the autonomy of EU associations. This latter factor appears to be much more significant for associations endowed with employer-representative capacities. Some associations without this factor, such as the EU Committee, are almost dependent upon the presence of such offices in Brussels to function. Here it is a positive factor, though given that virtually all such members have this presence it is not a factor of variation.

- The *Collective Cloak*. Business-wide associations take up general business environment and sometimes controversial and difficult issues for their members, both in public profile and in policy-making, that any one member might struggle with on their own. For instance, business-wide associations, by nature, deal with employer issues that are heavily contested. They may also be used by members to engage public opinion in a way in which no one company could wish to, or no one sector association would be able to on its own. One interview respondent in a leading position in one of the associations reviewed in this chapter commented that 'members give you the crap to deal with'.

- The *Common Enemy* factor, in that business-wide employer associations are deeply motivated in their formation and development by worker organisation through trade unions.

- *Threat of Exit* and *Extent of Evaluation Undertaken* is structurally lower where business-wide associations are endowed with formal capacities as employer-representative organisations. It is also not a factor of variation in these circumstances, justifying a lower weighting that with sectoral associations.

- *Benefits of Membership*, the *Costs of Non-Membership* and *Autonomy from Members* are structurally influenced by the role and extent of the association in employer-related functions, on the whole positively in the first two and negatively with the last one. *Trust between Members* may, however, be enhanced through increased intra-member contact.

- The *Costs of Non-Membership*, *Benefits of Membership* and *Association used for Membership* are also likely to be enhanced by business-wide associations whose appeal is based on the quality and breadth of the network. Reliance upon the association for formal sources of information, however, is likely to be reduced, in that members satisfy their sector-specific requirements from elsewhere. *Access to Other Organisations* may be less of a factor informing membership of business-wide associations than it is for sectoral associations, although UEAPME is an exception in developing NORMAPME.

- *Membership Density* is more significant for business-wide associations whose authority stems from the claim to represent such a constituency.

On the basis of the above discussion, the identification and weighting of factors for business-wide associations might look something like that recorded in Tables 5.4 (for those endowed with formal employer representative capacities) and 5.5 (for those without).

Table 5.4 Business-wide associations (with employer representation capacities): factor weightings and factor association with governability

Weighting	Association with governability (+ or −)
5	
'Common enemy'	+
Autonomy from members	+
Trust between members	+
Membership density	+
4	
Counter-lobbying by members	−
Prone to lowest-common-denominator positions	−
Membership for costs of non-membership	+
Membership for benefits of membership	+
Collective cloak	+
Degree of firms of similar size 4	+
Member/non-member activity in Brussels 1*	+
Member/non-member activity in Brussels 2	−
3	
Association used for lobbying	+
2	
Extent of evaluation undertaken	−
Threat of exit	−
Quality of network	+
1	
Association used by members for formal information	+

*See 'member activities in Brussels' on p. 144. This factor has both positive and negative associations with governability, and can thus be treated separately.

With these variations shown in Tables 5.4 and 5.5, the results obtained for cross-sectoral business associations are shown in Table 5.6 (with employer-representative functions) and Table 5.7 (without such functions).

These results accord both with the impressions gained from data collection and the wider literature, with the exception that the method employed clearly does not do justice to the European Round Table of Industrialists. Perhaps it is best to conclude that this organisation is too unique in concept to be evaluated by the criteria of governability identified here, but to emphasise the highly governable nature of the organisation by virtue of its exclusivity, the commonality of firm size and ideology, and its ability to cherry-pick issues. But this is a minor departure from the contribution of this chapter in assessing EU business-wide associations, and in developing a methodology to assess them.

Table 5.5 Business-wide associations (without employer representation capacities): factor weightings and factor association with governability

Weighting	Association with governability (+ or −)
5	
Autonomy from members	+
Trust between members	+
4	
Counter-lobbying by members	−
Prone to lowest-common-denominator positions	−
Membership for costs of non-membership	+
Membership for benefits of membership	+
Degree of firms of similar size	+
Quality of network	+
Extent of evaluation undertaken	−
Threat of exit	−
3	
Association used for lobbying	+
Membership density	+
Collective cloak	+
Member/non-member activity in Brussels	+
2	
'Common enemy'	+
1	
Association used by members for formal information	+

Table 5.6 Business-wide (employer) associations: variations in governability

Factor	UEAPME		UNICE	
	Simple	Weighted	Simple	Weighted
'Common enemy'	4	20	5	25
Autonomy from members	4	20	2	10
Trust between members	5	25	3	15
Membership density	3	15	4*	20
Counter-lobbying by members	3	12	2	8
Prone to lowest-common-denominator positions	4	16	2	8
Membership for costs of non-membership	3	12	5	20
Membership for benefits of membership	5	20	4	16

Table 5.6   Continued

Factor	UEAPME		UNICE	
	Simple	*Weighted*	*Simple*	*Weighted*
Collective cloak	4	16	5	20
Degree of firms of similar size	4	16	2	8
Member/non-member activity in Brussels 1**	4	16	4	16
Member/non-member activity in Brussels 2	3	12	2	8
Association used for lobbying	5	15	3	9
Extent of evaluation undertaken	4	8	5	10
Threat of exit	5	10	5	10
Quality of network	3	6	4	8
Association used by members for formal information	5	5	3	3
Average	4	14.4	3.5	12.4

* This is an increase of 1 from the values recorded in Chapter 4, as a result of further evaluation.
** See 'member activities in Brussels', p. 144.

Table 5.7   Business-wide associations without formal employer-representative structures: variations in governability

Factor	AMCHAM-EU		ERT		EUROCHAMBRES	
	Simple	*Weighted*	*Simple*	*Weighted*	*Simple*	*Weighted*
Autonomy from members	3	15	2	10	3	15
Trust between members	4	20	4	20	3	15
Counter lobbying by members	4	16	4	16	2	8
Prone to lowest-common-denominator positions	4	16	4	16	1	4
Membership for costs of non-membership	4	16	2	8	3	12
Membership for benefits of membership	4	16	5	20	1	4
Degree of firms of similar size	4	16	5	20	2	8
Quality of network	5	20	5	20	4	16
Extent of evaluation undertaken	3	12	2	8	2	8
Threat of exit	3	12	3	12	4*	16
Association used for lobbying	3	9	4	12	1	3
Membership density	3	9	2	6	2	6
Collective cloak	5	15	1	3	3	9
Member/non-member activity in Brussels	4**	12	4	12	1	3
'Common enemy'	4	8	3	6	2	4
Association used by members for formal information	4	4	1	1	3	3
Average	3.8	13.5	3.21	1.9	2.3	8.4

* An increase of 1 from the values recorded in Chapter 4, as a result of further evaluation.
** *Ibid.*, this factor works in a supportive way for this association.

6 Conclusions

In order to understand the governability of EU business associations, an essential first step is to appreciate the type of organisations they are, and the influences exerted by the environment in which they operate. In this concluding chapter, these key factors are summarised ahead of the other main influences on governability identified by the research on which this book has been based, and the contribution lent to methodology. The focus of these conclusions is to identify and assert the main findings, rather than to re-rehearse the ways in which they have been arrived at, or to aim to list once more every single causal factor explaining variation in governability. The richness of detail can be found in other chapters. One factor is, however, worth restating at this point, and that is that the focus of this book is to examine how the EU environment influences the governability of EU business associations, and to identify the principal causes of variation of governability – defined in Chapter 1 as their ability to unify their members' interests and to secure goal compliance.

TRUE TO TYPE: THE SPECIAL CHARACTER OF EU BUSINESS ASSOCIATIONS

A 'business association' conjures up a variety of concepts among readers, often quite differentiated by cultural setting. Those from countries with a Germanic basis to their language,[1] and from parts of Latin America, are likely to think of an organisation that is closely involved in mechanisms of public and private governance, often involved in regulating the environment in which they operate, delivering order and intertwined with the state machinery. Readers from these countries are likely to be familiar with the idea that a business association can bind and discipline its members to comply with its collective goals. In short, business associations are important intermediaries between the state and civil society in these countries, based on and expressing (in Germanic society at least) cherished values such as order, hierarchy, discipline, obedience and authority. 'Corporatist' arrangements are familiar to readers from these countries. Whilst it may have been an extremity of the quest for an empire in the era involved, a striking finding of Schneiberg and Hollingsworth (1991) reported in Chapter 1 is

---

[1] Hereinafter, for the purpose of shorthand, 'Germanic-speaking', although the longer phrase in the main text of 'a Germanic basis to their language' is designed to encompass Nordic countries and to some extent the Netherlands, as well as Germany, Austria and much of Switzerland.

that in 1938 nearly 50 per cent of Germany's industrial output was subject to price and production controls which were devised and managed by trade associations acting through the devolved authority of government. In Latin America, business associations in some countries are just as intertwined with the state in the present day, bearing significant responsibilities for organising and regulating markets, policy implementation and economic development (Doner and Schneider, 2001a), or even in sustaining corrupt regimes in return for economic favours (Rettberg, 2001).

Those from the Anglo-American world are likely to have different word associations for business interest organisations, and much lower expectations of the functions performed by them. Although some UK trade associations have performed historic roles as cartels, and a select few play roles in economic management that involve binding and disciplining members so as to maintain collective agreements with governments, such cases[2] are exceptions. They are on the whole much less important actors in civil society than in the Germanic countries. More typically, they are one among a number of actors active in a more pluralistic type of political system, albeit it as elites. These tendencies are even more pronounced in the USA, where they are more likely to be 'lobbyists' than 'interest intermediaries', and where business associations are deeply influenced by the vigour and culture of 'anti-trust' legislation. These factors influence the range of functions that associations undertake, the relationship with and behaviour of their members, and the size of the organisations in the different countries. Business associations in the Germanic-speaking world are, on the whole, much larger than their Anglo-Saxon counterparts, and are invested by their members with the capacities to bind and discipline individual members for the collective good. In Chapter 3, the example was provided by Pestoff (2000) of substantial, automated 'direct debit fines' levied by Swedish associations on findings of guilt by transgressors. Such an example is hardly imaginable in the case of EU business associations.

In all of these cases, the associations are 'children of their universe'; that is, products of the political systems in which they are embedded. The fragmented EU political system does not possess the 'stateness' to 'licence' associations to undertake monopolistic functions of control that would, in turn, make them significant intermediaries. In short, the EU is not a corporatist system of interest intermediation, but a pluralist system of interest representation in which there is a lobby 'free for all', in which associations can be more or less bypassed by those of their members who have the resources to do so, and where the institutions of political authority in the EU freely receive all comers. This is not an encouraging environment for business associations to operate in. There is no domain in which relations between business and government are conducted wholly through an

---

[2] The pharmaceuticals and advertising domains are among the principal ones.

associational intermediary in the EU. Deprived of a principal source of associational coherence and appeal – that of state patronage – EU business associations turn to specialism as a means of finding common positions. This specialism, in turn, limits their utility to EU political institutions seeking collective opinion that embraces the entire constituency likely to be influenced by a set of measures. In political systems where business associations are patronised by state authority, associations can afford a wider spectrum of membership because their reduced ability to reach to common platforms at a high level of specificity is offset by the value placed on membership by state patronage. In short, in the EU political system there is a triumph of the 'logic of membership' over the 'logic of influence' (Chapter 3).

Whilst EU business interest associations are more similar in concept to those in the Anglo-American world than the Germanic world, they are on the whole even less-developed than their UK counterparts. In both the Germanic and Anglo-Saxon worlds, business associations take on substantial membership-services functions, sometimes to such an extent that the political representation function is almost secondary. EU business associations are quite different animals. They are built around a narrow range of functions geared around the needs of their members to manage their political environment, and to network, with very few providing significant membership-services functions. There are a number of consequences to this, both negative and positive. Among the former are those based around resourcing and autonomy and their ability to bring value to their members. Among the positive aspects of the principally political and network foci of EU business associations are included ease of collective action. These are reviewed in turn below.

Resources, Specialisation and Autonomy

The narrow functions of EU business associations means that they have a low level of resources, and in many cases substantially less than their best-endowed members. To compound the problem, a substantial amount of the resources of EU business associations are taken up with translation requirements. These relativities mean that EU business associations tend to be overdependent upon their members for resources, and in consequence lack autonomy. The depth of the concept of autonomy can be gauged from its link to 'institutionalist' theories of integration, in that these concepts focus on the ways in which the perceptions of those who participate under their umbrella are constructed by these institutions. As was argued in Chapters 1 and 3, an association needs to have autonomy from its members in order to be able to bring value to them. Those that are too closely controlled by their members become a mouthpiece for their short-term demands, while those that have acquired some autonomy from their members' short-term demands have the flexibility to participate in policy-making with EU institutions. In acquiring this property, associations are able to bring value to their members. A cause and a consequence of this autonomy is the ability to construct a sense among their members as to what their long-term interests are. That is, the association is constructing the preferences of its members, rather than being a prisoner of them. It may withstand short-term member pressures in order to undertake their long-term interests.

To be able to undertake this delicate task, an EU association needs to avoid capture by any one specialised interest, to exceed its members' appreciation of EU public affairs, to have an independent supply of resources of funding and expertise, a decision-making structure which provides insulation from control by any one member, and highly skilled leadership. In general, their low levels of resourcing and lack of independence of resources mean that EU associations struggle to have all of these qualities, and, in the most extreme cases, become in the words of McCann cited in Chapter 3 'mere conduits of communication'. The high degree of specialism common to EU business associations means that they are too closely tied to the interests of their members, whereas associations with a more encompassing reach across different types of interests are more insulated from the demands of any one specialised constituency. This is one advantage that business-wide organisations such as UNICE have over narrow, highly specialised associations representing the interests of, say, vegetable protein or natural sausage casing manufacturers.

Because the functions of EU business associations are narrowly centred on those of political representation, they are dependent upon membership subscriptions for their incomes, and do not tend to have an independent supply of 'own resources' from the sale of other services that might commonly be found among national trade associations. Many EU associations are also young and have not built up substantial reserves or property interests in their own premises; rather, as relative latecomers to Brussels, many are victims of high property rents rather than owners of property which acquired later value through booms. This makes some dependent upon facilities provided by their members.

A consequence of this low level of resourcing also includes the commonplace practice of using secondments from members. In turn, this may undermine the key quality of trust that other members are prepared to invest in their association, such as handing over potentially sensitive information. As Coleman argues, as well as needing an independent and secure supply of financial resources, associations need the related ability to develop their own independent source of expertise, including staff, in order to increase the dependence upon them by others. Once this independence is acquired, associations can draw upon the information from their members to supplement their own resources, rather than to rely upon them (Chapter 3).

Associations that have the visible approval of state authority have the ability to keep their distance from their members. By the other token, associations also need to keep a distance from their 'state' interlocutors in order to preserve their autonomy, a problem in highly corporatist systems such as Austria. Few EU associations ever get close enough to the EU institutions to run this risk.

Transaction Costs

Transaction costs can be broadly defined as the costs of doing business (Chapters 1 and 3). Associations can reduce these costs, and arise partly as a result of doing so, often in circumstances of changes to the structure of competition originating in either markets or politics. In regulating transaction costs, business associations can bring high added value to their members. EU associations can, and in some cases do, undertake some of the functions of regulating transaction costs identified in the quotation taken from Hollingsworth, Schmitter and Streeck (1994) cited in Chapters 1 and 3. However, their focus as political and network organisations mean that they undertake much fewer of these than do associations in other settings. In addition, a key point is that EU business associations are limited in the scope of transaction costs they can regulate by the severity of EU competition policy, and DG Competition has not been slow in monitoring the activities of these associations (Chapter 3).

The structure of EU competition can therefore be disruptive for associability. Deregulatory politics can distribute benefits and costs narrowly, such as large firms standing to gain from open markets and smaller firms likely to lose from the enhanced competition that liberalisation brings. Such a fragmentation of interests produces competitive interest-group politics (Wilson, 1995), and stasis within associations in which these different interests are represented. Large firms with sufficient resources to dedicate to EU public affairs management are disruptive to EU associations. Among other factors which can also make EU associability and consensus-building in EU associations difficult is the grounding of EU competition in mutual recognition, which can unleash competition between national standards. Competition can be managed without the use of associations, and there are European structures such as product standardisation which can help business do this. In all these respects, the EU environment of competition is disruptive to associability (Chapter 3).

Fewer Collective-Action Problems

A further consequence of the narrowness of scope of EU business associations is that the range of 'collective-action problems' in EU business associations is less than in national associations. This is because members who are already politically active (either national associations or large firms) have established these organisations to undertake a specific function for them, and they do not require any special incentives to participate. The membership constituency (a relatively small number of national associations, or large firms) is much narrower than is often sought by national associations, who often need to appeal to a large constituency of potential (often SME) members. Whilst 'reasons' for participating in these organisations can be identified and classified as 'incentives', these 'incentives' play a less significant role in the dynamics of EU business associations than they do in national associations, because they exist to perform a narrow range of functions. In addition to this deductive analysis, both the quantitative and qualitative evidence is particularly strong in indicating that participation and continued membership is a mixture of normal political behaviour and habit for their members (Chapter 4). There was very little evidence of membership evaluation during the 150 or so member interviews, and a good deal of evidence of the 'normal political behaviour' perspective in the verbatim comments reproduced in Chapter 4.

There is a final factor in the general environment of EU business associations that is worth including in a summary of their common caricature, and which is not a product of their specialisation upon political and network functions. Despite a tendency towards direct company representation, most EU associations still include national associations among their membership, and a majority of them are, still, associations of national associations. This factor alone significantly conditions their governability. Those associations which draw authority from their claim to represent a wide constituency can be expected to be more prone to 'lowest-common-denominator' positions than are highly specialised exclusive associations, and they should not be evaluated unfavourably for undertaking the purpose for which they were intended. These associations have constitutional rules that are designed to make them consensus-driven, and without a high degree of state patronage it is unrealistic to expect them to deliver a high specificity of common opinion. On its own, however, this factor has been sufficient to inspire the creation of associations that, following the logic of finding cohesion from specialisation discussed earlier, are built around the needs of their members for delivering quicker, collective opinion at a high level of specificity. However, this latter capacity does not necessarily imply a higher degree of governability. Invariably, these organisations are based on a small number of large firms, which tends to reduce associational autonomy. Additionally, these organisations, like their federated counterparts, for reasons explained in the first section of this concluding chapter, do not display any ability to bind their members and to discipline them for non-compliance.

EXPLAINING VARIATIONS IN THE GOVERNABILITY OF EU BUSINESS ASSOCIATIONS

The analysis undertaken thus far in this concluding chapter has focused upon the general conditions facing most EU business associations. As such, factors like those of the environment of multi-level governance, EU competition policy, and low resources *relative to their members* are not sources of great variation in the governability of EU business associations. There are, of course, some variations in the impact of these, such as differences in the dispersal of authority across policy areas, but the similarities are greater than the variation. Indeed, the limited extent of differences in the impact of these factors means that they are not sufficient on their own to explain variation. What are the principal sources of variation? Chapters 4 and 5 present quantitative and qualitative evidence taken from data collection conducted among 50 EU business associations and 150 of their members as the basis to draw conclusions to this question, together with the literature review conducted in Chapter 3.

Taken as a whole, the domain-specific associations in the sample of associations taken in this study had a high degree of specialisation and a low degree of autonomy. These factors are related, in that specialisation leads to low membership numbers and associations that are closely controlled by their members, and consequently lack autonomy. Nonetheless, there were significant patterns of variation. 'Families' of closely related factors for domain-specific associations appear to be:

- *Overcapacity, the degree of competition* and *the extent of concentration* within a sector, where the presence of high overcapacity coupled with a low degree of competition and a relatively high degree of concentration appears to be a highly significant independent (i.e. causal) variable. It is no accident that EU associations such as CEMBUREAU, the European Broadcasting Union and EUROFER, all associations that have featured in EU competition-policy cases, are among the top quartile of highly governable associations. ACE, placed first and second in the two segments of Table 4.3, represents members from a sector that has also featured strongly in a competition-policy case, while its principal member has been the subject of a substantial competition-policy fine.
- *The cost of non-membership, but only in conjunction with the benefits of membership*, and related factors such as the use of the association for lobbying, and a low degree of counter-lobbying. Without the presence of the 'benefits of membership', the 'cost of non-membership' factor can be a cause of low governability in that the principal use of the association by members

may be as a 'spoiler' or potential 'spoiler', such as to make sure that the association does not take up a damaging position for them. Somewhere in between these also fit the factors 'low threat of exit' and 'extent of evaluation'. While these latter factors varied little, where variation did arise the effect appears to be substantial.

Once again, the presence of these as a 'family' of factors are a significant independent variable.

- *The degree of specialism, together with 'issue-niche' organisations* – each very strongly associated with governability, with one a subset of the other rather than combination factors. As has been indicated, a high degree of specialism enables cohesion in an association, and may be both a cause and a consequence of trust.
- *Autonomy, the degree of trust between members and between the members and the secretariat.* The degree of trust between members appears to be related to the extent to which the members of an association operate in lowly-populated and perhaps exclusive environments. In consequence, it is linked to the factors of degrees of overcapacity and concentration. It is thus related to the structural settings in which members compete, including factors such as new technology developments, which is in turn related to the stage in the product cycle. Other factors governing the exclusivity of the circles in which members operate are the institutional settings in which they participate.

Trust between members is also related to the degree of independence of resources of an association. An association heavily dependent upon the resources of particular members, such as secondments, is likely to create problems of intra-member trust.

High trust between the members and the secretariat is a factor that can only be built up over time and earned by the General Secretary (see Chapter 5). High 'trust' in an association can create the conditions for a high degree of autonomy, although as is evident from the earlier discussion in this chapter the extent of autonomy is heavily dependent upon resource independence and degree of specialisation, which is in turn related to other clusters of factors such as degrees of concentration.

- The degree of regulation is clearly a consideration, although this concept requires substantial refinement to be of value. Associations may be formed to seek or to oppose regulation. A high degree of regulation may result in a low threat of exit, but that may be to restrict the costs of non-membership rather than the benefits of membership. Different types of regulation produces different effects upon the configuration of interests, depending upon the distribution of costs and benefits, and can result in competitive politics. There is a relationship here with the factors 'a common enemy' and the 'collective cloak', in that to be cohesive the factor has to be perceived in the same way as the members.

Two factors that were expected to be strongly associated with governability were those of a 'common enemy', and 'the degree of firms of similar size'. Of surprise to the author was that associations where these factors were strongly present were highly disbursed throughout the four quartiles of associations in Table 4.3. This does not suggest that they can be dismissed as factors of independent significance, but it does suggest that they may be qualified by the presence of other factors. Clues to what these other factors might be come from an analysis of the contributory factors of governability in business-wide associations.

Chapter 5 examined the factors of variation among business-wide associations, and the extent to which causal factors of governability variation differ in their impact from domain-specific associations. A differing impact factor common to all business-wide associations concerned the issue of proximate member offices. Whilst there are costs and benefits of these, the benefits in all cases appear to outweigh the costs of a loss of autonomy, and in at least one case the presence of proximate members provides the foundation of the organisation.

Key factors of differentiation between business-wide associations were those of the design purpose of the association (breadth or selectivity of constituency), and the possession or absence of an employers' representation function. In the case of associations that were built on their encompassingness, and their functions as an employer-representation organisation, fluctuation considerations of governability in comparison to domain-specific associations were:

- *Degrees of membership density.*
- *The extent of the 'common enemy', in conjunction with the 'collective cloak',* in that these factors provide the foundation for such organisations. Thus, the *'cost of non-membership'* is also higher, with a consequent reduction in importance of the 'threat of exit' and 'degree of evaluation undertaken', in that these are organisations that no serious national member could contemplate leaving. However, as discussed in relation to domain-specific associations, in order to act positively on governability the 'cost of non-membership' factor has to be coupled with the 'benefits of membership'.

For business-wide organisations that were not built on their encompassingness or an employers' representative function, other factors distinguished them from domain-specific associations in the ways they impacted upon governability. These centred on a family of related factors, including:

- *trust*;
- *the degree of firms of similar size*; and
- *the quality of the network.*

The success of organisations such as the European Round Table of Industrialists and the EU Committee of the American Chamber of Commerce are built on the possession of these qualities. Of interest, however, is that the success of these two organisations is not dependent upon the autonomy of the secretariat. Both of them are member-driven organisations with the secretariat playing a supporting rather than leading role. This may be specific to the unique and exclusive profiles of these two organisations, built around the most powerful company interests imaginable. The fact that these associations are not tied to the interests of a small number of members means that their lack of autonomy does not prevent governability. This factor also helps explain the importance of 'trust', in that member companies are drawn from a variety of sectors and are not necessarily in competition with one another. Trust is also a product of the shared ideology of these firms in liberal markets, and it is this factor that explains why 'the degree of firms of similar size' matters with these type of associations when it does not seem to be strong enough on its own with domain-specific associations.

THE METHODOLOGICAL LEGACY

As well as identifying the principal factors of governability of EU business associations, this comprehensive study has sought to develop and refine methodological instruments to examine them. It has generated the most substantial public data-set of quantitative and qualitative evidence about EU business associations that is currently available, with claims of generalisability to the population of these organisations. It is therefore worth taking some moments of summary reflection as this book draws to a close.

The study started off by generating a list of candidate factors of governability, through deductive and inductive methods. Among the latter were included primary data collection amongst a sample of 49 EU business associations, broadly matched against the universe of such organisations, including interviews with a variety of actors including association staff (49) and members/non-members (151). These candidate factors were then examined inductively for their suitability, including the use of a process of 'weighting'. This process of weighting has been arrived at through a deductive process that was then assessed inductively. A number of challenges to these weightings was provided by this process, such that a future study could attribute the highest weightings to the principal factors discussed in this concluding chapter. The mix of deductive and inductive processes was chosen so as to build on the strengths of each. Deductively-based models on their own, derived from logical reasoning, are a researcher's best friend and worst enemy at the same time, in that while they provide a framework, the researcher tends to find evidence of what they are looking for while missing factors they are not searching for. Inductive, 'on-the-ground' methods help resolve these latter difficulties, though when there is overreliance on these methods they can deliver research findings that are 'hit and miss'. Both methods have been incorporated in the research design of this book. In Chapter 2, it was argued that 'whilst it is difficult to distinguish between the origin of knowledge as deductive or inductive, it is possible to deliberately seek to incorporate each concept in a research design, systematically investigating hypotheses (deductive), and using hypotheses as synthesis in itself (inductive)'. On this basis, a research design has been created for both domain-specific associations, and one that is tailored to the context in which business-wide associations operate, whether based on representativity and employer functions, or those that lack these functions.

As to the results obtained about governability, the 'families' of factors identified above provide some reassurance that the methodologies have been appropriate, while the general consistency of the data with the deductive analysis is another source of reassurance. There are 'holes' in the data, such as more information being required on membership density, though this is a study in itself, while a perfect data-set might have involved undertaking more member interviews for certain associations. No study would be advised to claim completeness; but a fair claim has been made to match the aspirations suggested by the title of this book, to get inside the EU business associations, to examine how the EU environment influences the governability of EU business associations, and to identify the principal causes of variation of governability.

Appendix: Members of EU Business Associations – Interviews

Organisation:

Interviewer:

Respondent:

Date:

Time/Final Rating:

Summary:

1 Which sectors of business activity would you describe yourselves to be active in?
2 Which, if any, formal EU Business Associations are you currently a member of?
3 Do(es) these(is) memberships represent all of your product market interests in the EU?
4 (If more than one) Can multiple membership be explained by functional divisions only? Are there competing or complementary organisations?
5 Are there any you have left? Why?
6 Are you a member of any of the (a) formal, and (b) informal, x sectoral business organisations? What do you hope to achieve by this?
7 Apart from your membership of associations, how else, if at all do you achieve your EU public affairs representation needs? (If via own office, how many staff work there, or which how many are non admin/secretarial)?
8 Do you undertake your own direct representation with the EU institutions? If yes, do you undertake this in the sectors where you have associational membership?
9 In general, do you think there is anything like a trend for the EU institutions to talk more to firms than to associations?
10 Does your sector have a specific regulatory regime designed by the EU?
11 (a) To what extent has the sector covered by association x been the subject of de/re/ regulation? When has this mainly occurred?
    (b) What changes, if any, has this brought to associability in your sector?

From this point on, I would like to talk to you particularly about your membership of
x association ...

12 Business associations perform a number of tasks for their members, from networking through to lobbying. On a scale from 1–100, how much does your membership
of *x* association fulfil your EU-related lobbying needs?

13 Some associations are particularly prone to the 'lowest-common-denominator' problem. To what extent is this true of *x* association?

14 Some say that the ability of an association to go beyond lowest-common-denominator
positions depends upon the characteristics of the particular sector, whereas others
would say that it depends more upon the management and leadership of an association.
Which of these factors do you think is a more important influence? Please comment ...

15 Why are you a member of your *x* association? Can you articulate for me your membership reasons, in priority order 1, 2, 3?
    (1)
    (2)
    (3)

16 (If not clarified already) If not for lobbying, how do you secure this function?

17 How active a member are you? Some members prefer to take a back seat, while
others like to try and drive the association as far as possible. On a scale from 0 (least
active) to 100 (very active), how would you rate yourselves?

18 On a scale from 0 (none) to 100 (completely), how much do you rely upon your
trade association for an information service?

19 For some, the most important reason to be a member of their association is to make
sure that it does not take up a damaging position for them. For others, this is not an
important factor in continued association membership. To what extent does this drive
your membership of *x* association?

20 In general, some EU trade association memberships seem to be on an 'insurance-
policy' basis – that is, the emphasis is on the costs of non-membership rather than
the benefits of membership. How accurate is this to describe
    (a) your membership of *x* association (if not covered by q. 17 already)
    (b) the membership of others, as far as you can assess, in *x* association ...

21 And the collective cloak? To what extent is membership of the EU trade association
because of the need to have company/nat. assoc. positions undertaken under the
name of the sector-wide body?

22 (a) Would you describe the industrial activities represented by *x* association as having a
         clear and cohesive identity, or would you describe them as somewhat fragmented?
    (b) How does your answer to (a) affect the ability of *x* association to act on behalf of
         its members?

23 Would you say there is a clear identity to the economic activities represented by *x*
association, or would you say that the association covers economic activities which
are somewhat fragmented?

24 To what extent are there very specialised associations representing similar types of
interests in *x* industrial domain?

25 To what extent are the interests covered by *x* association contested by public interest
groups? Is this a source of coherence for *x* association?

26 Can you tell me how much, in total, you spend on your affiliation to *x* association?

27 Can you tell me what you do to evaluate your membership of *x* association? Is there
a periodic evaluation?

28 Has there been a debate in your association about the format (types of members – associations, and firms) it should take? When was this debate, and how, if at all, has it been resolved?

29 Can you describe the way in which common platforms are built in your association? In particular, would you characterise platform building in your association as informal, or highly formalised?

30 (a) What does x association do best?
   (b) What does x association do less well?
   (c) What, if any, changes could be made to the structure of x association to make it more effective?

31 Some EU associations have a European identity because they have a 'European line' to argue in world trade negotiations, etc. Are these factors a source of coherence in x association?

32 To what extent does the sector covered by x association have a population of firms of similar size?

33 Are there many SME firms in the sector? To what extent does x association represent small firms in the sector?

34 (a) Many industries have become more concentrated in recent years. To what extent is this true of the principal sector(s) to which you belong?
   (b) And how has this affected x association?
   (c) Has it made agreement in x association more or less difficult?

35 (a) To what extent is there now competition in your sector? Where does the competition come? (prices, differentiated products, etc.)
   (b) Is the competition chiefly within, or outside, the EFTA? How does the nature and intensity of competition in the sector covered by x association?

36. Some industries are divided by competing technologies, where firms have different interests according to the technologies upon which their products are based. Is this a source of division in x association?

Bibliography

AMCHAM-EU (EU Committee of the American Chamber of Commerce), 'Member List', http://www.eucommittee.be/Pages/fsprof9.htm

Balanyá, B., Doherty, A., Hoedeman, O., Ma'anit, A. and Wesselius, E. (2000) *Europe Inc.* (London: Pluto Press).

Bennett, R. (1997a) 'The Relation between Government and Business Associations in Britain: An Evaluation of Recent Developments', *Policy Studies*, 18(1): 5–33.

Bennett, R. (1997b) 'Trade Associations: New Challenges, New Logic?' in R. Bennett (ed.), *Trade Associations in Britain and Germany* (London, Anglo-German Foundation): 1–11.

Bennett, R.J. (1998) 'Business Associations and their Potential to Contribute to Economic Development: Re-exploring an Interface between State and Market', *Environment and Planning A*, 30(8): 1367–87.

Bennett, R.J. (1999) 'Explaining the Membership of Sectoral Business Associations', *Environment and Planning A*, 31: 877–98.

Bennett, R.J. (2000) 'The Logic of Membership of Sectoral Business Associations', *Review of Social Economy*, LVIII(1), March: 17–42.

Betts, P. (2001) 'The Quiet Knights of Europe's Round Table', *Financial Times*, 20 March 2001: 16.

Boléat, M. (1996) *Trade Association Strategy and Management* (London: Association of British Insurers).

Boléat, M. (1999) 'The Changing Environment for Trade Associations', paper prepared for presentation to the International Hotel and Restaurants Association Congress, Durban, 19 October.

Boléat, M. (2001) *Good Practice in Trade Association Governance* (London: Plaza).

Branch, A. and Greenwood, J. (2001) 'European Employers: Social Partners?' in H. Compston and J. Greenwood (eds), *Social Partnership in the European Union* (London: Palgrave).

Browne, W. (1977) 'Organizational Maintenance: The Internal Operation of Interest Groups', *Public Administration Review*, 37, January–February: 48–57.

Browne, W. (1990) 'Organized Interests and their Issue Niches: A Search for Pluralism in a Policy Domain', *Journal of Politics*, 52(2), May: 477–509.

Bruyn, S.T. (1991) *A Future for the American Economy: The Social Market*, (Stanford, Stanford University Press).

Butt Philip, A. (1985) 'Pressure Groups in the European Community', Working Paper no. 2, London, University Association for Contemporary European Studies (UACES).

Butt Philip, A. and Gray, O. (1996) *Directory of Pressure Groups in the European Union* (Harlow: Cartermill).

Butt Philip, A. and Porter, M. (1997) 'Business Alliances, Network Construction and Agenda Definition: Recent Development in Lobying Activities in Brussels and Strasbourg', paper presented at the Fifth Biennial International Conference of the European Community Studies Association, Seattle, 29 May to 1 June.

Caporaso, J. (1974) *The Structure and Function of European Integration* (Goodyear: Pacific Palisades).

Cawson, A. (1992) 'Interests, Groups and Public Policy Making: The Case of the European Consumer Electronics Industry', in J. Greenwood, J. Grote and K. Ronit (eds), *Organized Interests and the European Community* (London: Sage): 99–118.

Claveloux, D. (1993) 'Talking to the EC: Consultation, Lobbying and Openness: A Background Briefing for the June 15 Conference at the Palais des Congrès in Brussels' (Brussels: Forum Europe).

Coen, D. (1997) 'The Evolution of the Large Firm as a Political Actor in the European Union', *Journal of European Public Policy*, 4(1), March: 91–108.

Coleman, W.D. (1985) 'Analysing the Associative Action of Business: Policy Advocacy and Policy Participation', *Canadian Public Administration*, 28(3): 413–33.

Coleman, W.D. (1988) *Business and Politics: A Study of Collective Action* (Kingston, McGill: Queen's University Press).

Coleman, W. and Grant, W. (1984) 'Business Associations and Public Policy: A Comparison of Organisational Development in Britain and Canada', *Journal of Public Policy*, 4(3), August: 209–36.

Commission of the European Communities (1992) 'An Open and Structured Dialogue Between the Commission and Special Interest Groups', Brussels, SEC (92) 2272 final.

Compston, H. and Greenwood, J. (2001) *Social Partnership in the European Union* (London: Palgrave).

Cowles, M.G. (1995) 'The European Round Table of Industrialists: The Strategic Player in European Affairs', in J. Greenwood (ed.), *European Casebook on Business Alliances* (Hemel Hempstead: Prentice Hall): 225–36.

Cowles, M.G. (1996) 'The EU Committee of AmCham: The Powerful Voice of American Firms in Brussels', *Journal of European Public Policy*, 3(3), September: 339–58.

Crouch, C. (1998) 'Adapting the European Model: The Role of Employers' Associations and Trade Unions', in and G. Huemer, M. Mesch and F. Traxler (eds), *The Role of Employer Associations and Labour Unions in the EMU: Institutional Requirements for European Economic Policies* (Aldershot: Ashgate): 27–52.

Doner, R.F. and Schneider, B.R. (2001a) 'Business Associations and Economic Development: Why Some Associations Contribute More than Others', *Business and Politics*, 2(3), November: 261–88.

Doner, R.F. and Schneider, B. (2001b) *The New Institutional Economics, Business Associations, and Development* (Geneva: International Institute for Labour Studies).

Eichener, V. and Voellzkow, H.V. (eds) (1994) *Europäische Integration und verbandliche Interessenvermittlung* (Marburg: Metropolis Verlag): 349–83.

ERT (European Roundtable of Industrialists) (2001a) *Opening up the Business Opportunities of EU Enlargement* (Brussels: ERT).

ERT (2001b) 'Members', http://www.ert.be/pc/enc_frame.htm

ERT (2001c) 'Achievements: Highlights of ERT Activities', http://www.ert.be/pg/eng_frame.htm

EU Committee (2001) *News Sheet*, January 2001 (Brussels: The EU Committee of the American Chamber of Commerce).

EurActiv.com (2001) 'Project: Serving the Community of EU Actors', http://www.euractiv.com/cgi-bin/eurb/cgint.exe/82075?11&1011=boutus1

EUROCHAMBRES (1998) *Annual Report* (Brussels: Eurochambres).

Euroconfidentiel (1998) *World Directory of 9300 Trade and Professional Associations in the EU* (Genval: Euroconfidentiel).

Euroconfidentiel (1999) *World Directory of 9300 Trade and Professional Associations in the EU* (Genval: Euroconfidentiel).

European Commission (1996) *Directory of Interest Groups* (Luxembourg: Office for Official Publications of the European Communities).

European Commission (2001) 'Directory of Interest Groups in the European Union', http://europa.eu.int/comm/secretariat_general/sgc/lobbies/index_en.htm

Gardner, J. (1991) *Effective Lobbying in the European Community* (Dordrecht: Kluwer).

Gosman, A. and Forman, D. (2001) 'Industry Associations: Adapt or Die', *Corporate Public Affairs*, 11(1): 1–4.

Grande, E. (1996) 'The State and Interest Groups is a Framework of Multi-Level Decision Making: the Case of the European Union', *Journal of European Public Policy*, 3, 5, September: 318–38.

Grant, W. (1990) 'Organised Interests and the European Community', Paper prepared for presentation to the 6th international colloquium of the Feltrinelli Foundation, Corton, 29–31 May 1990.

Gray, O. (1998) 'The Structure of Interest Group Representation in the EU: Some Observations of a Practitioner', in P.-H. Claeys, C. Gobin, I. Smets and C. Winand (eds), *Lobbying, Pluralism and European Integration* (Brussels: European Interuniversity Press): 281–303.

Gray, O. (2001) 'Self Regulation of Advertising: The Internet Issue', paper prepared for a workshop on 'Lobbying the EU: Changes in the Arena', Leuven, 24–5 January 2001.

Gray, P. (1998) 'The Scientific Committee for Food', in M.P.C.M. van Schendelen (ed.), *EU Committees as Influential Policymakers* (Aldershot: Ashgate): 68–88.

Gray, V. and Lowery, D. (1997) 'Reconceptualising PAC Formation: It's Not a Collective Action Problem and it May be an Arms Race', *American Politics Quarterly*, 25(3).

Greenwood, J. and Aspinwall, M. (1998) *Collective Action in the European Union: Interests and the New Politics of Associability* (London: Routledge).

Greenwood, J., Grote, J. and Ronit, K. (eds) (1992) *Organised Interests and the European Community* (London: Sage).

Greenwood, J. (1995) *European Casebook on Business Alliances* (Hemel Hempstead: Prentice-Hall).

Greenwood, J. (1997) *Representing Interests in the European Union* (London: Macmillan – now Palgrave).

Guéguen, D. with Rousseff, B. (2000) 'French We Are ... but How Unfrench Can We Go?', *Public Affairs Newsletter*, November: 10–11.

Haas, E. (1958) *The Uniting of Europe: Political, Economic and Social Forces, 1950–1957* (Stanford: California University Press).

Hayward, J. (1975) 'Employer Associations and the State in France and Britain', in S.J. Warnecke and E.N. Suleiman (eds), *Industrial Policies in Western Europe* (New York: Praeger): 118–47.

Hollingsworth, J.R., Schmitter, P.C. and Streeck, W. (1994) *Governing Capitalist Economies: Performance and Control of Economic Sectors* (Oxford: Oxford University Press).

Institut des Sciences du Travail (1999) 'Report on the Representativeness of European Social Partner Organisations', Part 1, http://www.europa.eu.int/comm/employment_social/soc-dial/social/index_en.htm

Kirchner, E. (1981) *The Role of Interest Groups in the European Community* (Aldershot: Gower).

Landmarks Publications (2000) *European Public Affairs Directory 2001* (Brussels: Landmarks).

Lehmkuhl, D. (2000) 'Under Stress: Europeanisation and Trade Associations in the Member States', *European Integration Online Papers*, http://eiop.or.at/eiop/texte/ 2000–014a.htm

Litvak, I. (1982) 'National Trade Associations: Business–Government Intermediaries', *Business Quarterly*, Autumn: 34–42.

Lowi, T. (1964) 'American Business, Public Policy, Case Studies and Political Theory', *World Politics*, 16: 677–715.

Macdonald, A. (2001) *The Business of Representation: The Modern Trade Association Forum* (London: Department of Trade and Industry/Trade Association Forum).

Martin, C.J. (1997) 'Mandating Social Change: The Business Struggle over National Health Reform', *Governance*, 10(4), October: 397–428.

McCann, D. (1995) *Small States, Open Markets and the Organization of Business Interests* (Aldershot: Dartmouth).

McLaughlin, A.M., Maloney, W.A. and Jordan, A.G. (1993) 'Corporate Lobbying in the European Community' *Journal of Common Market Studies*, 31(2), June: 191–212.

McLaughlin, A. and Maloney, W. (1999) *The European Automobile Industry* (London: Routledge).

Mizruchi, M. (1992) *The Structure of Corporate Political Action* (Cambridge, Mass.: Harvard University Press).

Müller, H.W. (1997) 'Thinking Small, Acting Big', *European Voice*, 3(20), 22–28 May: 14.

Newton, K. (2001) 'Trust, Social Capital, Civil Society, and Democracy', *International Political Science Review*, 22(2): 201–14.

North, D. (1990) *Institutions, Institutional Change and Economic Performance* (Cambridge: Cambridge University Press).

Olson, M. (1965) *The Logic of Collective Action* (Cambridge, Mass.: Harvard University Press).

Olson, M. (1971) *The Rise and Decline of Nations* (New Haven: Yale University Press).

Orgalime (1996) *A Strategy for Orgalime* (Brussels: Orgalime).

Pedler, R. (ed.) (2001) *European Union Lobbying* (London: Palgrave).

Pedler, R. and van Schendelen, M.P.C.M. (eds) (1994) *Lobbying the European Union: Companies, Trade Associations and Issue Groups* (Aldershot: Dartmouth).

Pestoff, V. (2000) 'Europeanisation and Globalisation of Business Interest Associations – Exit Provides Two or More Voices, but Implies No Loyalty', paper delivered at a workshop on 'Europeanisation and its Impact on National Forms of Business Associability', Florence, 1–3 June 2000.

Pijnenburg, B. (1998) 'EU Lobbying by Ad-Hoc Coalitions', *Journal of European Public Policy*, 5(2): 302–21.

Rettberg, A. (2001) 'The Political Preferences of Diversified Business Groups: Lessons from Colombia (1994–1998)', *Business and Politics*, 3(1), April: 47–64.

Sabatier, P. (1992) 'Interest Group Membership and Organisation: Multiple Theories', in M. Petracca (ed.), *The Politics of Interests* (Boulder: Westview): 99–129.

Scharpf, F. (1988) 'The Joint-Decision Trap: Lessons from German Federalism and European Integration', *Public Administration*, 66(3): 239–78.

Schmitter, P.C. and Streeck, W. (1981) *The Organization of Business Interests: Studying the Associative Action of Business in Advanced Industrial Societies*, Max Planck Institute for the Study of Societies, Discussion Paper 99/1.

Schmitter, P.C. (1992) 'The Consolidation of Democracy and Representation of Social Groups', *American Behavioural Scientist*, 35(4–5), March/June: 422–49.

Schmitter, P.C. (1997) 'The Emerging Europolity and its Impact Upon National Systems of Production', in J. Rogers Hollingsworth and R. Boyer (eds), *Contemporary Capitalism: The Embeddeness of Institutions* (Cambridge: Cambridge University Press): 395–430.

Schneiberg, M. and Hollingsworth, J.R. (1991) 'Can Transaction Cost Economics Explain Trade Associations?', in R.M. Czada and A. Windhoff-Heritier (eds), *Political Choice: Institutions, Rules and the Limits of Rationality* (Frankfurt: Campus): 199–231.

Sidjanski, D. (1967) 'Pressure Groups and the European Community', *Government and Opposition*, 2(3): 397–416.

Smith, M. (1998) 'UNICE Attempts to Do Less, Better', *Financial Times*, 25 August: 10.

Staber, U. and Aldrich, H. (1983) 'Trade Association Stability and Public Policy', in R.H. Hall and R.E. Quinn (eds), *Organizational Theory and Public Policy* (Beverley Hills: Sage): 163–78.

Streeck, W. and Schmitter, P.C. (1985) *Private Interest Government* (London: Sage).

Streeck, W. and Schmitter, P.C. (1991) 'From National Corporatism to Transnational Pluralism: Organized Interests in the Single European Market', *Politics and Society*, 19(2): 133–64.

Traxler, F. (1991) 'The Logic of Employers' Collective Action', in D. Sadowski and O. Jacobi (eds), *Employers' Associations in Europe: Policy and Organisation* (Baden-Baden: Nomos): 28–50.

Traxler, F. and Schmitter, P.C. (1994) 'Associations in the Euture Euro-Policy', paper prepared for presentation at the XVIth World Congress of the International Political Studies Association (IPSA) Berlin, 21–24 August 1994.

Tyszkiewicz, Z. (2001) 'National Members and their EU Associations', in J. Greenwood (ed.), *The Effectiveness of EU Business Associations* (London: Palgrave).

UEAPME (European Association of Craft, Small and Medium-Sized Enterprises) (1997) *Annual Report 1997* (Brussels: UEAPME).

UEAPME (1998) *Our Vision: A Europe for Craft and SMEs* (Brussels: UEAPME).

UNICE (Union of Industrial and Employers' Confederations of Europe) (2001) *Preliminary UNICE Position on European Governance* (Brussels: UNICE).

UNICE (1997) *Statutes* (Brussels: UNICE).

Union of International Associations (1998) *Yearbook of International Organizations* (Frankfurt: Bowker-Saur).

van Apeldoorn, B. (2001) 'The European Round Table of Industrialists: Still a Unique Player?' in J. Greenwood (ed.), *The Effectiveness of EU Business Associations* (London: Palgrave).

van Schendelen, M.P.C.M. (1998) *EU Committees as Influential Policymakers* (Aldershot: Ashgate).

van Waarden, F. (1991) 'Two Logics of Collective Action? Business Associations as Distinct from Trade Unions: The Problems of Associations as Organisations', in D. Sadowski and O. Jacobi (eds), *Employers' Associations in Europe: Policy and Organisation* (Baden-Baden: Nomos): 51–84.

White, D. (1997) 'Dealing with Trade Associations: A Two Way Process', in R. Bennett (ed.), *Trade Associations in Britain and Germany* (London: Anglo-German Foundation): 74–7.

Williamson, O. (1996) *The Mechanisms of Governance* (Oxford: Oxford University Press).

Wilson, J.Q. (1995) *Political Organizations* (Princeton: Princeton University Press).

Index